HOW TO HANDLE MAJOR CUSTOMERS PROFITABLY

DEDICATION

To Sue, for her good humour and patience

and

to Michelle and David

How to Handle Major Customers Profitably

ALAN MELKMAN
BSc(Eng), MSc(Econ)
of Marketing Improvements Limited

A Gower Press Workbook

Published by
Gower Press, Teakfield Limited,
Westmead, Farnborough, Hants., England

Melkman, Alan
    How to handle major customers profitably.
    1. Customer relations   2. Marketing management
    I. Title
    658.8'12   HFS415.5

ISBN 0 566 02097 1

Printed in Great Britain by Biddles Limited, Guildford, Surrey

Contents

Preface

More and more suppliers are now operating in a market place where relatively few customers account for a large proportion of their total sales. This phenomenon is common and although it may be deplored by many, the clock cannot be turned back. The perfectly competitive market place characterised by many suppliers selling to a multitude of customers, on which much traditional economics is based, is in many markets a thing of the past. This change means that a few major customers are often the cornerstone of a company's prosperity. That this poses a threat is indisputable and it requires a fundamental appraisal of the total approach to the market which is often not fully recognised by the supplier.

Over the last ten years I have worked with a large number of companies spanning nearly all sectors of industry from high value capital goods to fast moving consumer goods, from repeat industrial consumables to consumer durables. This experience, coupled with that of my colleagues within Marketing Improvements, means that knowledge of most types of business situations across Europe and the other continents has been gained. By conducting training courses and carrying out consultancy assignments in many industries, Marketing Improvements has built up a large bank of knowledge and expertise. From these broadly based observations of how companies handle their major customers and in discussing their methods of operation with all levels of management and staff, it has been possible to draw certain conclusions. These are:

1 All companies are aware that their major customers differ from their smaller ones in their methods of operation, the time taken to obtain their business, and the importance of these major accounts to the overall success of the company.

2 Very few suppliers *act* as though they had carefully considered these differences and developed their policy, organisation, planning mechanisms, and systems accordingly.

3 There is no one best solution, the adoption of which will ensure the effective handling of major customers. Each company must develop its own policy, organisation structure and so on. Even in the same industry different approaches have been found to be successful for different suppliers.

While learning from the many companies with whom I have worked, senior management in these organisations have asked me questions about the practices of other companies and how these relate to their own situation. The following questions are most frequently asked:

What sort of organisation structure is needed?

How can the efforts of a number of staff selling to and servicing major customers be co-ordinated, both nationally and internationally?

What knowledge and skills do sales and sales support staff require and how should they be trained?

How can the dependence of the company on a handful of major customers be reduced?

What proportion of total sales revenue and profit should the top ten customers account for?

What written material exists to give guidance on how major customers should be tackled?

In nearly all cases it has been possible to give positive and constructive advice to help answer all these questions, except the last one. Books exist on negotiation techniques, contract handling and selling to large customers. Very little has been written that discusses all the main aspects of dealing with major customers, largely because it is often difficult to consider major customers totally separately from the rest of the business. This is so because, in spite of many significant differences, there are also many similarities between large and small customers. Both types will have some similarity in buying needs, purchase similar products, possibly be called on by the same salesman, receive standard invoices and statements and so on. Thus, much of the general literature concerned with business planning, marketing planning, sales force management, organisation structure and sales techniques also has some relevance to major customers. Besides this general literature, there are some books on certain techniques such as negotiation which tend to be more relevant to large customers than smaller ones. Even when a manager has read these books he is often left with the feeling that he understands each particular element but not how to fit them all together to help him develop his total approach to major customers.

The purpose of this book is to bring together in one place all the most important aspects of major customer handling. Some aspects may be familiar to the reader, many may be new. As such it is intended to be both a reference and a practical guide to help the manager critically review his current effort towards his larger customers.

Although written primarily for senior managers including the managing, marketing and sales directors, because of the impact of major customers on all aspects of the business, the book will also be of interest to the production, technical and finance departments. In a desire to provide the manager with a back-up reference handbook it has been necessary to include some standard material with which the senior manager will already be familiar, and which should be being implemented by the sales manager and salesman. This material will be useful to the senior manager in refreshing his understanding and in helping him check the current practices in his organisation.

The book is not solely a marketing book, or a book on selling; it is a business book. This is because the supplier must consider his total organisational response to major customers if he is to handle them effectively. That such an approach must include discussion on the customer interface with production, technical development, finance and so on is self-evident.

The book is in three parts. Chapters 1 to 3 discuss the framework within which activity towards major customers must be considered. They look at the role of, the company policy towards, and the organisation structure needed to handle, major customers. The middle three chapters consider the planning which must take place to maximise the return obtained within the overall policy set and describe the necessary information systems. The last three chapters discuss the implementation of the plans and the systems and control mechanism required.

In some sections the reader will see that the subject material is as applicable to the rest of his customers as it is to major customers. The reason for including this material is either that it is more important to large customers, for example customer profitability analyses, or that the conclusions derived therefrom will lead to a separate course of action. The procedures and techniques detailed in each chapter have been drawn from the 'best practices' being carried out by operating companies.

At the end of each chapter is a checklist summarising the most important points. By completing this checklist the manager can develop an action plan to help in bringing about the necessary changes.

The book is based on the premise that since major customers are important and often vitally so, then it is worthwhile for management to devote time and effort to considering how they can most effectively be handled. In attempting to help the manager in this task the book bridges the gap between the general marketing and sales literature available covering the relevant functional activities and the books on specific techniques such as sales forecasting, financial techniques, negotiation, which are of relevance to major customers.

It is recommended that the reader refresh his knowledge on the general aspects of each subject area if he finds that the introductory sections in each chapter are inadequate for him. Conversely, if the reader is fully conversant with a specific subject area then he may care to omit the opening sections of the chapter and concentrate on the specific applications to major customers.

Finally it is suggested that the senior manager may care to use certain sections of the book to provide either a check on, or a basis for, current operating methods such as training and systems. To facilitate this it will probably be useful for these sections to be made available to operational staff.

Essentially this workbook is a practical tool to assist managers in carrying out their jobs. This does not mean that it shies away from dealing with concepts; rather, that devices such as checklists, analysis formats, have been included to enable the manager to deal with them and relate them to his own situation. Clearly it is not possible to deal with every conceivable company/customer situation and adaptation may be necessary. Where this is necessary, I would very much appreciate hearing about particular instances so that the book may be improved and updated when the opportunity occurs.

Alan Melkman
Marketing Improvements Ltd
London NW1
September 1978

Acknowledgements

A book such as this represents the distilled experiences and thoughts of many colleagues and clients. It is impossible to acknowledge fully their contribution to the development of this subject material and my debt to them is enormous. I wish to thank them all and to single out a few individually for their help.

In particular I would like to thank: Bernard Atkins, formerly of CPC Europe Ltd and now with Eley/IMI; Michael Wilson, MI's Managing Director, for his perseverance in reading through successive drafts of this book and his constructive comments; John Lidstone, MI's Deputy Managing Director, for the work he has carried out on 'Negotiation'; Mike Holliday for his constructive and commonsense approach to major customer profit and loss analysis; Peter Kirkby, MI's Director of International Operations, for initiating much of the work.

I would also like to thank many of our past and present consultants including Rod Fennemore, Anthony Lawler and Richard Taylor, whose hard and effective work for client companies has been of considerable assistance.

Finally, my thanks go to my wife, Sue, for her support and encouragement during the writing of this book, and to my PA, Sue Plummer and Ros Lewis.

A.V.M.

1
The role of the major customer

1.1 INTRODUCTION

At 10.00 a.m. on Monday 9 May 1977, the Chairman of Tesco Holdings Limited, the high-street multiple grocery company, made an important announcement. As from Thursday 9 June the company would cease to give Green Shield stamps to its customers and would embark instead on a new 'value-for-money' strategy. The statement was especially noteworthy since in many ways Green Shield had grown up with Tesco. The relationship started in 1963 had firmly established the trading stamp company and Tesco had been a major customer ever since. The termination of the agreement was a source of serious concern for Green Shield.

In 1972 a computer software company called NMW was formed to provide a service to the brokers and jobbers on the Manchester Stock Exchange. A year later, when the merger of the Provincial and London Stock Exchanges took place, the business faced considerable difficulties.

These two examples show companies in different industries who have come face to face with the opportunities and problems presented by major customers. Their experience is by no means unique.

In markets everywhere, from shipping to insurance, from agricultural equipment to grocery goods, major customers are an established fact of life for the seller. In some cases, such as a steam turbine manufacturer, the CEGB may well be its only customer in the UK.

Many other supplying companies who utilise a distribution network, whether it be hardware goods, automotive replacement parts or agricultural supplies, are facing a concentration of power in the distributive channels. Figure 1.1 shows how, for example, power has been concentrated in retail grocery channels since 1961 to the extent that multiples now account for nearly half of all grocery business in the UK. Similar trends are apparent throughout Europe and the USA, and Table 1.1 shows how large retailers are expected to increase their dominance in all EEC countries.

Before examining how the supplier should tackle the challenge presented by major customers, by looking at each aspect in detail, it will be useful to establish some basic terminology and background theory. This first chapter therefore examines the role and general operating mechanisms of the major customer. In particular, it defines what is meant by a major customer, looks at why they are important and shows how their impact on the suppliers' business can be quantified, at least in part. It goes on to discuss how major customers operate and what they expect from their suppliers, the types of buying situations they face, and the various stages they go through when they are buying. Finally, changes in the buyer/supplier relationship are examined, particularly with regard to their impact on the supplier and on the role of his sales force.

Some of the material in this chapter is applicable to all customers and not just major ones. The reason for including such material is that most companies, if they consider these matters at all, do so implicitly. However, major customers are so important that

1

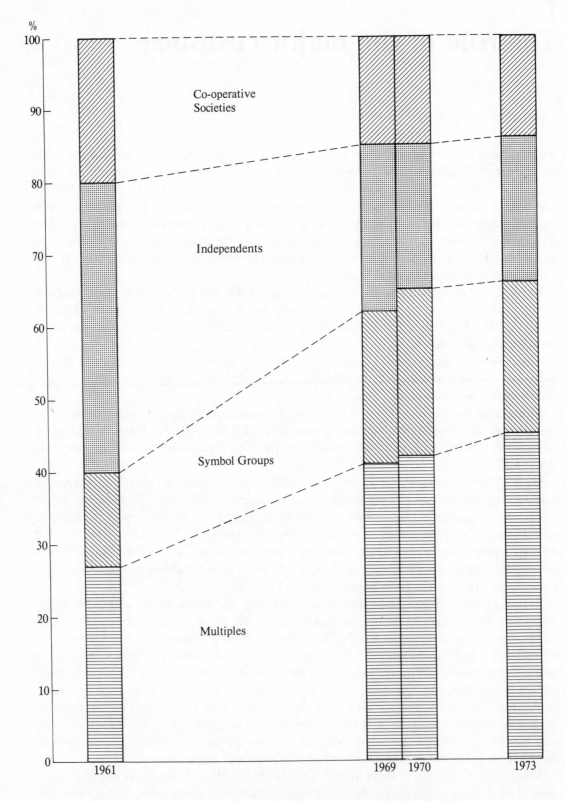

Figure 1.1   Proportion of total UK grocery trade by outlet type
Source: Census of Distribution

these factors need to be considered explicitly in relation to each one. A crude analogy may be the situation faced by a gardener tending his lawn as compared with his prize roses. The lawn could represent a large number of small customers. He does not need to examine each blade of grass for he knows that provided the lawn is mowed regularly and given the correct nutrients, and undesirable growths are expelled, it will give acceptable results. The prize roses could represent the small number of major customers. Each bush must be tended individually. The gardener must understand the growing mechanism of the plants and how each will react to different stimuli.

Table 1.1   Percentage of large scale retailers in total retail trade, by country

Country	1962	1971	1980 (estimate)
Belgium	15.6	21.3	30–35
Denmark	17.0	23.2	30–35
France	19.4	28.7	35–40
Germany	23.4	32.6	40–45
Ireland	12.7	21.7	30–35
Italy	4.8	8.8	15–20
Luxembourg	2.5	3.2	4–5
Netherlands	24.2	29.1	40–45
UK	45.5	50.3	58–63
Average	18.3	24.3	31–36

Source: Distributive Trades in the Common Market – HMSO
(Reproduced with permission of the Controller of HMSO)

1.2   WHAT IS A MAJOR CUSTOMER?

A major customer is a customer who takes a significant proportion of a supplier's business. In extreme cases a 'significant proportion' may be 100 per cent, but more usually it is considerably less, and it can be said that almost any customer taking more than 5 per cent of a company's business is major.

Another way of identifying a major customer is to calculate what effect the loss of that customer will have on the seller's business. If the effect on sales and profits is significant, then the customer can be classed as major. Figure 1.2 provides a convenient format for listing these accounts and their recent turnover. It is normally least difficult to rank major customers on the basis of invoiced sales, although for a capital goods company, order input may be more appropriate. The company names should be listed in the first column, and last year's sales in the next. The four columns that follow enable changes in the size ranking of the customers to be recorded alongside their turnover. If there are any significant customers who were once important but are so no longer then the table should be extended to enable them to be included in earlier years. This exercise will show how the importance of the top twenty customers has changed over the last five years as a proportion of the total company sales. If they appear to be taking up an increasing proportion of sales then detailed consideration of the material in this book will contribute to the company's future success.

On completing the exercise using Figure 1.2 some readers will find that there have been significant changes in the rankings of their top twenty customers. This raises a number of questions:

Customer name	Turnover (order input) £								
	Last year	2 Years ago		3 Years ago		4 Years ago		5 Years ago	
	T/O	T/O	rank	T/O	rank	T/O	rank	T/O	rank
1									
2									
3									
4									
5									
6									
7									
8									
9									
10									
11									
12									
13									
14									
15									
16									
17									
18									
19									
20									
A Total £									
B Total company turnover £									
A/B %									

Figure 1.2   Trends in customer turnover

1 Was the change planned?
2 Have key customer contacts left?
3 Have the customers themselves substantially increased or decreased in size?

The answers to these questions will show how vulnerable the relationships with major customers are. In particular, does the supplier have (a) a broad base of contacts within his major customers, (b) a number of his own staff familiar with each large account, (c) a specific plan of where he is going?

1.3 WHY ARE MAJOR CUSTOMERS IMPORTANT?

The analysis carried out using Figure 1.2 will have shown who the major customers are and quantified their importance. However, sheer volume of turnover is only one facet of their importance, others include the following.

1 Providers of base load business for the factories.
2 Generators of profit.
3 Offering opportunities for significant expansion.
4 Providing the means of developing and testing new products on a limited tailor-made basis.
5 Giving the business an apparent stability (although on further examination this may prove illusory).

Major customers have always been important to the supplier, but there are indications that they are becoming even more so. This is due to a number of factors, now described.

Inflation, increasing costs and effect on distribution channels

Cost increases
One of the main reasons why large customers are becoming more important is cost increases. In particular, the cost of servicing small accounts has increased dramatically over recent years. Distribution costs, sales costs and administration costs have rocketed. This has led many companies to consider alternative, cheaper ways of servicing smaller customers, including: (a) telephone selling, (b) contract ordering, (c) mail order, (d) using a distributor/wholesaler.

The first three, telephone selling, contract ordering and mail order, reduce selling costs and in some cases distribution costs and are unlikely to have a significant effect on the mix of customers. Using a distributor reduces distribution costs but affects customer mix. For example, instead of, say, 500 small accounts, a company may have one distributor catering for their needs, who, in turn, becomes a large, often powerful customer.

Thus, large customers, particularly when they are members of a distributive chain, may be the only way a supplier can get the desired level of penetration into the market place to meet his marketing objectives at an acceptable cost level.

Distribution channels
To quantify the impact of using a variety of distribution channels it is useful to draw a product flow diagram through the distributive channels as shown in Figure 1.3. This particular example is for an automotive component supplier and simplifies the actual situation. There are basically five ways in which the components can reach the final user.

5

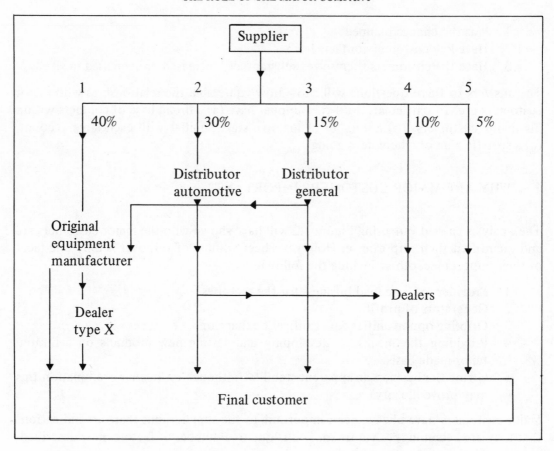

Figure 1.3 An automotive component supplier

Channel 1: via original equipment manufacturers. The components are sold to automotive and associated equipment manufacturers, who in turn sell direct to the final user or through a dealer (type X).

Channel 2: via distributors. The components are sold to automotive distributors who resell to the manufacturers in smaller volumes or to automotive dealers (garages) who use the product to replace worn parts. The automotive distributor also sells direct to the final customer (car owner).

Channel 3: via distributors. The components are sold to general distributors who resell to other applications of a general engineering nature. In turn they resell the components to OEM's (non-automotive) and other dealers who sell direct to the user. The general distributor also sells direct.

Channel 4: via dealers. The supplier also sells direct to dealers, where they are large enough to buy at least minimum order quantities, who in turn sell to the final customer.

Channel 5: direct from suppliers. Some customers, such as industrial companies running large transport fleets, buy in this way.

The analysis carried out by the supplier shows that Channel 1 accounts for 40 per cent of sales; Channel 2, 30 per cent; Channel 3, 15 per cent; Channel 4, 10 per cent; and Channel 5, 5 per cent. If it is further established from the analysis carried out using Figure 1.2 that five customers control four-fifths of sales in Channels 2 and 3 and a further four customers take up all of Channel 1, then over three-quarters (40 per cent + 4/5 x 45 per cent = 76%) of all sales are in the hands of nine customers. The analysis will also have shown how the importance of these nine customers will have changed over the last five years.

Clearly, not all the channels shown in Figure 1.3 will be relevant to every company, and where more complex channels of distribution are used these should be added to the diagram. Each supplier must develop his own distribution flow diagram.

By comparing Figure 1.3 with the major customer trends identified in Figure 1.2, it will be possible to see which distributive channels are increasing in importance, and which are dominated by relatively few major customers. If company objectives and marketing strategy dictate that these particular channels should become even more important, then the major customers concerned become vital to the continuing success of the business. In turn this will dramatically increase the risk to which a company exposes itself and should lead management to critically review its objectives and strategy.

Increasing order size

Another reason for the importance of major accounts to a company is that many suppliers perceive their future growth as coming from larger size orders. This is particularly so with industrial and service companies. For example, one manufacturer of high technology equipment selling to a wide cross section of industry foresees the bulk of his future growth coming from orders of £0.5 million or more, as opposed to a traditional average order size of around £20,000. Clearly this has implications for a supplier's total approach to its customers. For most organisations, however, the change in order size is not as dramatic; it may creep up almost imperceptibly. To establish how the average order size has changed over the last five years, the format in Table 1.2 may be used.

Table 1.2   Trends in average order size

	Last year	2 years ago	3 years ago	4 years ago	5 years ago
Average order value £					
Average order volume					

If average order size has changed significantly, a breakdown of Table 1.2 into each of the distributive channels identified in Figure 1.3 will go some way in explaining why order size is increasing.

Natural growth of customers

Mergers, takeovers and natural growth of companies have led to a process of concentration in many industries. Grocery retailing and electrical equipment are but two illustrations of a common phenomenon. In some cases this concentration has resulted from some companies being able to offer their customers better, more efficient or cheaper services or products. In others it has been caused by companies coming together either naturally or by government pressure. Legal changes such as the abolition of retail price maintenance have also played a part by enabling the larger customer who bought at cheaper prices to reduce his resale price and hence increase his competitive advantage.

1.4   HOW DO LARGE CUSTOMERS OPERATE?

There is clearly no set pattern in how large customers operate in relation to their suppliers. Numbers of studies have been undertaken by suppliers to establish buying patterns and buyer attitudes. There will be exceptions to any general rules, although the following will be useful.

Relationships with suppliers

Although large customers are generally tough, demanding buyers, it is not part of their function or in their own best interests to drive their suppliers out of business. On the contrary, they derive considerable benefit from working closely with their suppliers. This is particularly so in industrial markets where buyer and seller often co-operate to develop new products and applications. In fact, on occasions the co-operation is so close, with personnel from the buyer and supplier working together in a project team, that it is not unknown for a customer to patent products and systems developed by the team.

However, most successful buyer/seller relationships are developed on a basis of mutual trust. This requires that the supplying company earns the respect of the buyer in a number of ways: (a) knowledge and skills of the salesman, (b) technical service, (c) administrative efficiency. Thus, sales staff as well as the various functional specialists have to be able to discuss and understand a broad range of topics including: (a) technical aspects, (b) commercial aspects, (c) financial implications, (d) marketing implications, (e) production aspects.

Furthermore, to do an effective job the salesman must understand the difference between *selling* and *negotiation* and become well versed in the art of negotiating profitable sales.

The sales process often becomes more complicated and time consuming owing to three common problems associated with producing major sales.

1   Special design requiring research into the client's problems, needs, capabilities and expectations. This occurs across the whole spectrum of supplier types, from the food manufacturer going into own label products to the high value capital goods supplier designing for a particular application.
2   The supplier has to call on his own resources to develop the right design, to put together an effective sales proposal, and to convince a committee of practically-minded executives of the value of the proposals.
3   Once the order has been obtained, the supplier has to maintain a constant vigil to ensure correct delivery and installation, effective progressing of any order schedule, ongoing service and follow-up.

As one buyer in a large organisation put it, 'I don't just need a top-flight salesman to visit me, I want my supplier's total organisation to respond to my needs'.

Thus, the supplier's total approach and the resources he brings to bear on the large customer must be orchestrated to meet that customer's needs. These resources will include: (a) R and D, (b) order progress, (c) credit control, (d) design, (e) distribution, (f) marketing, (g) production.

Large company buying situation

The methods used by large buyers to reach and execute their buying decisions have been found to vary with the category of product or service being bought. The following three categories of purchase have been identified.

1   New purchase: a product or service which has not been purchased by the customer before.
2   Straight repeat purchase: the repurchase of products with which the buyer is familiar and has previous buying experience.
3   Modified repurchase: stands between the other two in terms of its familiarity to the buyer. A change in packaging or specification by the supplier would fall into this category.

New purchase

Typical examples include a retailer taking on a new product or brand, a farmer buying a new milking parlour, an engineering company buying a new numerically-controlled machine tool, and a chemical company building a new process plant. Generally, this represents the most complex buying situation, involving the largest number of company decision makers and buying influences. The complexity arises because the company is involved in a new buying experience, which is equivalent to a problem-solving challenge of some magnitude requiring considerable information. The customer will probably choose from as great a number of alternative supplier offerings as he can reasonably handle.

The purchase decision is unlikely to be made by any one person, although it may be the buyer's signature on the official order. Usually the decision will emanate from either a formal or informal committee including members of relevant functions. For a multiple retailer this will include buyers, senior operations management, marketing and finance staff. For a chemical contractor this will include purchasing staff, design engineers, product engineers. It is not unusual for a buyer to canvass the opinion of the relevant influencers in his own organisation. This can be formalised to the extent of circulating a rating form on which are listed the various elements of the supplier's offer. The various factors are weighted and the weighted scores totalled. The highest scoring supplier is most likely to get the order. Figure 1.4 shows an example of one such form. The weighting factors are determined subjectively by the buying organisation in relation to their estimate of what is important in choosing a supplier for the particular range of products or services. In the example shown in Figure 1.4 the customer considers the factors related directly to the supplying company's ability and performance and the product itself to be of primary importance. Sales and sales support are of secondary importance. The weightings may change for a different class of products or services.

It is important for the supplier to find out the factors and weightings being used by the buyer so that he can tailor his presentation accordingly.

The new purchase situation presents the supplier's salesman with a considerable challenge. To the extent that he can pass on useful information, offer a comprehensive solution, or reduce apparent risk, he will receive more sympathetic consideration from the buyer. It may often be necessary for the supplier to form a sales team which comes together on an *ad hoc* basis and is made up of staff with the necessary knowledge and skills to interlock with the purchasing team. This adds a further dimension to the sales interface requiring clear role definition on the supplier's side which will be discussed in Chapter 8.

Straight repeat purchase

This is at the opposite end of the scale from the new purchase. Typical examples are stock ordering by the supermarket manager, typewriter ribbon buying by the office

Supplier Rating Form

			Rating Scale:		
SUPPLIER	A:	A D Jenks Ltd	Very good	4	
	B:	Tefler & King Ltd	Good	3	
	C:	A & M Company Ltd	Below average	2	
	D:	P J Products Ltd	Poor	1	
	E:	A N O Ltd			Date: July 1978

Supplying company	A	B	C	D	E
Supply capacity	3	4	4	2	4
Financial stability	4	4	2	3	4
Technical support	3	3	2	3	3
Service support	2	3	3	4	3
Management quality	1	2	4	3	3
Trade union relationships	1	4	4	3	3
Regional warehouse location	3	4	4	2	3
sub total	17	24	23	20	23
Weighted sub total (× 1.07)	18.2	25.7	24.6	21.4	24.6

Service	A	B	C	D	E
Delivery reliability	3	1	4	3	4
Loan machine availability	2	1	2	3	4
User manuals	4	3	4	3	3
Part delivery follow-up	2	1	4	4	3
Schedule control	2	1	4	2	3
Price negotiation	4	4	4	3	3
sub total	17	11	22	18	20
Weighted sub total (× .83)	14.1	9.1	18.3	14.9	16.6

Products	A	B	C	D	E
Quality	3	4	4	3	3
Product range availability	4	4	1	3	4
Reject rate	2	3	4	3	4
Packaging	2	4	4	4	3
Guarantee	4	4	2	3	4
sub total	15	19	15	16	18
Weighted sub total (× 1.5)	22.5	28.5	22.5	24.0	27.0

Sales support	A	B	C	D	E
Salesman's knowledge	4	3	4	2	1
Productiveness of sales calls	1	2	3	2	1
Speed and accuracy of extra information	2	4	4	3	2
Prompt submission of quotes	3	2	4	3	2
Effectiveness of complaint handling	3	2	4	2	1
sub total	13	13	19	12	7
Weighted sub total (× 1)	13	13	19	12	7

Weighted total	67.8	76.3	84.4	72.3	76.3

Notes

Weights:	Supplying company	30
	Products	30
	Service	20
	Sales support	20
	Maximum total score	100

Figure 1.4 Supplier rating form

10

manager, machine oils purchasing by the factory manager and replacement parts acquisition by the factory maintenance supervisor. The company chooses from suppliers on its 'authorised list', giving consideration to its past buying experience with the suppliers. Salesmen from new companies have a difficult job to break into this situation.

Typically, only one man, usually the 'buyer', will take the purchasing decision with only a limited amount of influence from other personnel. Buyer 'inertia' is an extremely important factor and the salesman's main hope in breaking the established buying pattern lies in convincing the buyer and/or key influencers that new features or terms justify converting the straight repeat purchase situation to a modified repurchase one.

Modified repurchase
This stands between the other two in terms of complexity, information requirements, number of alternatives sought and time taken. Such situations can occur, for example, when a supplier tries to impose a price increase and the customer begins to re-examine the alternatives available. Another example might be that of a food processing company considering increasing its manufacturing capacity by adding additional processing lines, or the office manager considering the purchase of additional typewriters. Where a contract comes up for annual review this also represents a modified repurchase situation.

The buyer will typically take into account the views of his colleagues on an *ad hoc* basis. Generally the decision will be taken by the buyer who will be seeking to: (a) ensure that the new offering has significant benefits in terms of cost, delivery, performance, (b) keep his colleagues contented, (c) minimise risk of the new item letting him down. The type of purchase situation may vary considerably between different customers, depending on the customer characteristics. One buyer, for example, may always get competitive quotations, another may always use one supplier.

It is useful to identify the type of purchase situation being faced with the top twenty customers since this has a significant effect on the nature and scale of the sales effort required and the time taken to obtain the order. Moreover, it will show where the supplier is in a defensive situation (straight repeat purchase) and where he must attack (new purchase). For some customers more than one category of purchase will be appropriate. This will be the case, for example, when a buyer stocks a number of products which he re-orders in a straight repeat purchase manner, but he will go through new purchase behaviour when considering a new product from the same supplier.

The buying stages

In structuring the sales approach to the major customer, the supplier should be aware of the stages that buyers go through in reaching and implementing their purchasing decisions. Typically, the buyer will go through eight steps as shown in Figure 1.5. Initially he will be stimulated into action by recognising he has a need, created by a problem or opportunity. For example, it may simply be that a machine in the factory has broken down and production is being lost, or, perhaps, an opportunity exists for the distribution manager to show his expertise by reducing costs. In either case, the buyer will move to step 2 and determine what products or services exist that will satisfy the fundamental requirement, i.e. getting production flowing or reducing distribution costs. In the former case the solution is simple: a replacement part. For the distribution manager a large number of alternatives will exist ranging from hiring management consultants to automating the warehouse. The buyer then moves to step 3 in specifying the product or services required and then to step 4 in searching for potential suppliers. Where a replacement part is needed this procedure can be carried out quickly since the part number can be specified and the supplier is already known. For the distribution analysis it is much more difficult and time consuming.

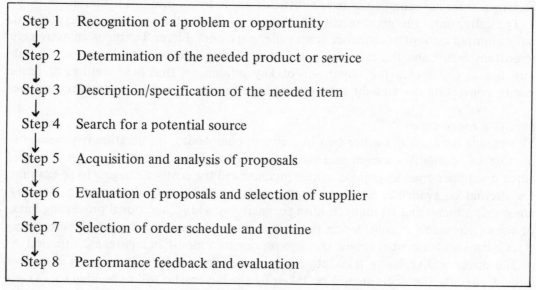

Step 1 Recognition of a problem or opportunity

Step 2 Determination of the needed product or service

Step 3 Description/specification of the needed item

Step 4 Search for a potential source

Step 5 Acquisition and analysis of proposals

Step 6 Evaluation of proposals and selection of supplier

Step 7 Selection of order schedule and routine

Step 8 Performance feedback and evaluation

Figure 1.5   The buying stages

Having located potential suppliers the buyer will move to step 5 and obtain a quote on a proposal and decide the most suitable supplier in step 6. This can be as informal as getting a price over the telephone or may involve the presentation and analysis of detailed written proposals.

Having placed an order, details such as delivery points, schedules and invoices will be agreed in step 7 and, once delivery has been made, in step 8 the performance of the product will be monitored and judged.

The speed with which a customer goes through each step and on to the next will vary according to the category of purchase. As the examples show, progress in the straight repeat purchase situation (machine spare part) is relatively fast. For the new purchase situation (management consultants) it will be slow and extensive.

The supplier, being aware of the various steps in the buying sequence, can tailor his selling effort to assist the buyer to move through each stage with a view to his making a favourable decision. For example, for some classes of spare parts which are sold through a large number of competing distributors/dealers, one of the main factors determining whether an order is obtained by any one dealer is the initial enquiry by the customer. When the machine breaks down, the customer will have a choice of which supplier to telephone. If a dealer can set up a mechanism which triggers the customer's memory in his favour and ensures he is contacted first, then he has an excellent chance of taking the customer through the typical straight repurchase situation to a successful conclusion. The dealer therefore should seriously consider developing a telephone sales operation which frequently contacts potential customers, so that when a machine breaks down, the foreman or manager immediately contacts the particular supplier who is uppermost in his mind. This quickly moves the customer through steps 3, 4, 5, 6 and 7.

Another example of where such a telephone sales system works is in the construction plant hire market. Here the supplier can offer only the type of plant he has available, i.e. that which he has not already hired out. Thus, each morning the major customers will be contacted to assess any needs for plant. This moves the customer from step 1, recognition of need, to step 7, selection of order schedule, very quickly.

1.5 CHANGES IN THE BUYER/SUPPLIER RELATIONSHIP

The trend towards larger customers, for the reasons identified earlier, has caused changes in the buyer/seller relationship. In many cases the power balance will have shifted in favour of the customer, although a significant degree of interdependence is likely to exist. For example, few major retailers can afford not to stock nationally advertised brand leaders whilst the gain or loss of one large multiple retail account can enable the packaged food supplier to acquire or lose national distribution. Similarly, the buyer of a machine may be tied into the supplier for the purchase of specific consumable items used on or with the machine, whilst a substantial proportion of the supplier's profit may depend on a few large customers using large amounts of consumables.

The change in the power balance between large buyer and seller has caused the supplier to redefine his relationship with his major customers in a number of ways:

Increased seller interest in the buyer's decision

Since the outcome of the major sale will often have an enormous impact on the supplier, he will seek to reduce the risk of failure. Generally this involves staying close to the buyer so as to gain further information during the decision-making period, particularly when the customer is going through a new purchase or modified repurchase situation. This can be a costly exercise and it is not unusual to have one man spending all his time looking after one large customer.

Increased buyer/supplier interdependence

There are many cases where a large customer has asked suppliers to recompute their prices since they appear too low. There is no merit in buying from a low bidder only to bankrupt him with the order incomplete. The wisdom of a supplier and customer entering into such a heavily dependent relationship is clearly questionable.

Typically, builders may quote prices that are too low in their eagerness to get a contract. The wise contractor or local authority will treat such quotations with care. Unfortunately it is still the case that many building jobs remain half finished because the builder has insufficient funds to complete.

Similarly, retailers like Marks and Spencer and the large catalogue mail order companies will ask for a re-quote if they suspect the supplier cannot reach the required quality standards at the quoted price.

Political considerations

In selling to a large number of small accounts, the supplier can treat each one as fairly similar requiring relatively little contact. However, where there are many inputs into the buying decision which the supplier must seek to influence, he will inevitably become enmeshed in the internal politics. He must be aware of these subtleties if he is to maintain good relationships with all concerned and achieve his sales objectives. He must be constantly aware of management changes and reorganisations and their implications for his offerings.

Top executive's role

Many companies operate on the principle that 'everybody in the organisation is a sales-man'. The chief executive or marketing director often makes it his business to meet top level customer staff towards the end of the sales process. This can be done in any number of formal or informal ways. His role will be to add authority and importance to the obtaining of the order and he will relate to the top level customer personnel on a businessman-to-businessman level, rather than a supplier-to-customer level.

Changing sales process

All that has been said so far clearly indicates that the sales process is becoming more complex. This requires new and vastly different sales methods and sales systems. The following qualities and requirements are particularly important for the salesman.

1 A much broader base of knowledge and skills than his counterpart of twenty years ago.
2 Ability to manage the resources available to him from within his company in selling to his large customers.
3 Thorough professional training. The old-fashioned, hard hitting, evangelical approach ceases to be of value in the face of an increasingly complex buying situation.
4 The availability of systems which provide information to enable a well thought out strategy to be planned and to yield information to ensure that the plan is implemented effectively.

Post sales involvement

The small customer is usually left on his own once the sale has been made. The large customer requires on-going servicing to ensure that the products and services continue to meet expectations and also to provide warning of possible new orders.

Remuneration

In the situation where the computer salesman can obtain an order which is larger than the total of all orders obtained by the calculating machine salesman during his whole sales career, it is necessary to re-examine remuneration policy methods. Typically, monetary incentive will not be centred around the amount of business obtained, since the salesman is often but one member of a team, but on how effectively he uses his limited time. This clearly requires a more sophisticated sales reporting and control system than the more traditional methods.

Timescale

The length of time taken to get a large customer is generally quite long, running into several years sometimes. This often requires considerable patience on the part of the supplier.

1.6 ROLE OF THE SALES FORCE AND SALES MANAGER

'The salesman is not dead, he's different.' The complexity of the major customer buying process means that the salesman's role becomes more important than ever before. This means that he must develop new knowledge and skills as outlined below.

1   Knowledge of the financial and operational needs of his *own* company and of the *customer's* business and how to apply that knowledge in his selling to major customers.
2   Analytical skills to plan long term mutually profitable customer strategies and to implement those strategies.
3   Managerial skills to enable him to 'orchestrate' the human and other resources available in implementing the plans for major customers.
4   Knowledge, skills and expertise to negotiate profitable business with key accounts.

With these skills in his 'kit bag' the salesman becomes more than an order-getter. He becomes a key factor in determining the company's success. The way in which he performs his job will probably have a greater impact on the company's profitability than almost any other function in the organisation.

Although it has always been fashionable to say that the salesman has been the manager of his geographic territory, this has only been so within very narrow and defined limits. It is much more true for the salesman selling to major customers who often has no clear, defined geographic territory, since he has more resources under his control and far greater numbers of decision variables to consider. He will often need to co-ordinate the activities of support personnel and negotiate prices/discounts.

Similarly, the sales manager's role has also changed. Although he still reviews such statistics as call rate, travelling distances and so on, he is much more concerned with what happens before, during and between sales calls. To this end, he will be responsible for developing his salesman's analytical, negotiation and planning skills. Each major customer, because of its size, will come under review and the manager will monitor the salesman's performance against an agreed activity plan.

1.7 SUMMARY

This first chapter has defined what is meant by a major customer, looked at why they are important, how they operate, trends in the buyer/supplier relationship and finally the changing role of the supplier's sales force in obtaining business from major accounts.

It is seen that large company buying methods vary with the category of the purchase they are making. The structure and complexity of this process varies likewise. Therefore the supplier must 'orchestrate' his sales effort so that it recognises the following:

1   The difference between the purchasing categories.
2   The mutual dependence of buyer and supplier.
3   Different combinations of purchasing categories that may be found among different major buyers.
4   Variation in the buying system, with a tendency to decrease in formality and complexity from the new purchase to the straight repurchase situation.
5   A reduction in the time taken to reach a decision from the new purchase to the straight repurchase situation.

In doing so, it is apparent that most of the factors are interrelated. By considering them as a whole, the supplier can ensure he has the appropriate structure, systems, strategy and staff to meet the challenge of major customers. Only those suppliers who upgrade their professionalism to match the power of the large customer can hope to maintain their profit position. This means that the total impact on the organisation should be analysed carefully by the senior manager. It is only by structuring all parts of the company to meet the big buyer's needs that success will be achieved.

In our experience only a minority of companies explicitly consider all aspects and only a few of them have developed a systematic approach to major accounts. Companies that have been successful have one main factor in common: they have recognised that their major customers differ from their smaller ones, not only in their scale of operation but also in their nature and in their individual importance to the business. Thus they have adapted their total response to take account of, and capitalise on, these differences.

The ensuing chapters show how this examination should take place and how the systematic approach should be developed based on the best practice evolved by successful companies.

Action planning checklist

Questions	Answers and action	Timing of action and evaluation
1 What is my company's definition of a major customer?		
2 What are the trends in sales to my major accounts over the last five years?		
3 What do the major accounts require of my company now that they did not five years ago?		
4 What changes have there been in the relative importance of my distribution channels over the last five years?		
5 How has average order size varied over the last five years?		
6 What future trends are likely?		
7 What type of buying activity takes place within each big account?		
8 What mechanisms exist within my company to enable effective co-ordination of all the necessary functions to occur?		
9 What weaknesses exist in these mechanisms and how should they be remedied?		

2
Establishing company policy

2.1 INTRODUCTION

Most suppliers, in the short term, are committed to their current customer mix. This particular mix will have resulted from company strategy decisions to attack certain markets. If a supplier's market is the petrochemical industry then he has little choice but to sell to the large oil companies. However, the resultant mix of customers may not be ideally to his liking. The supplier may feel that too many of his eggs are in one basket, and that this makes him too vulnerable. This raises a number of questions:

What should the company do?
How does it judge if it is too vulnerable?
What sort of customer mix would be satisfactory?

To answer these questions presupposes that the company has some sort of yardstick against which to judge, i.e. that it has established its *policy* regarding the mix of customers it wants.

This chapter looks at how such a policy should be formulated. The fact that a supplier may not be able to fulfil the policy guidelines in any, but the long term, does not invalidate the reasons for having such a policy. In the short term he may have to make do with his current customers and be grateful for the business they give. The development of the supplier's marketing and sales strategy will be directed towards the achievement of the desired goals dictated by the policy. This chapter first discusses a method for establishing the shape of a supplier's current customer mix (Pareto analysis) and then shows how it can be used to establish company policy, relating it to the company's long term objectives and marketing strategy. Therefore it will be of fundamental importance to the marketing director and general manager, as well as being of some interest to the sales manager or brand manager.

2.2 THE PARETO DISTRIBUTION

Pareto's Law is well known to most businessmen. First developed by the Italian economist Vilfredo Pareto at the end of the nineteenth century to describe the concentration of wealth and income in Italy, it can be applied to many different activities. Sometimes it is called the 80:20 rule, e.g. in most companies, eighty per cent of sales are accounted for by twenty per cent of customers (or products). A clear method of showing this diagrammatically is to draw a Pareto distribution. This is compiled by listing all customers in decreasing order of turnover and plotting the cumulative turnover related to the number of customers as shown in Figure 2.1. It is generally easier to use log graph paper to plot the curve as this saves space by foreshortening the scales. The Pareto distribution in Figure 2.1 shows that the top one hundred customers account for £4.6 million turnover. Doubling the number of customers to two hundred only increases turnover by £0.6 million to around £5.2 million.

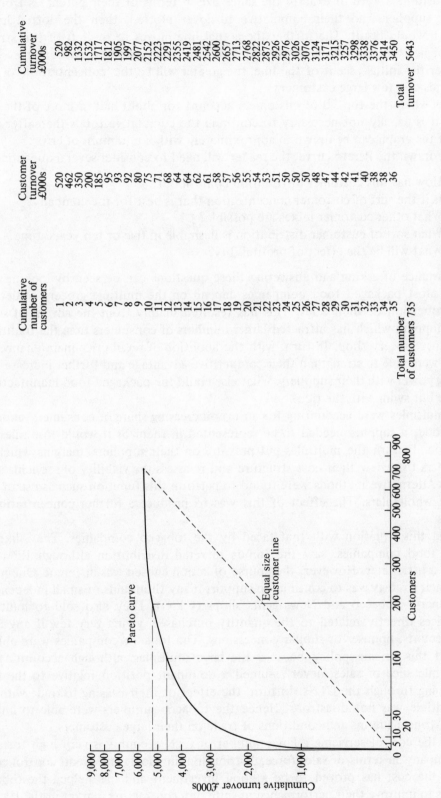

Cumulative number of customers	Customer turnover £000s	Cumulative turnover £000s
1	520	520
2	462	982
3	350	1332
4	200	1532
5	185	1717
6	95	1812
7	93	1905
8	92	1997
9	80	2077
10	75	2152
11	71	2223
12	68	2291
13	64	2355
14	64	2419
15	62	2481
16	61	2542
17	58	2600
18	57	2657
19	56	2713
20	55	2768
21	54	2822
22	53	2875
23	51	2926
24	50	2976
25	50	3026
26	50	3076
27	48	3124
28	47	3171
29	44	3215
30	42	3257
31	41	3298
32	40	3338
33	38	3376
34	38	3414
35	36	3450

Total number of customers 735

Total turnover 5643

Figure 2.1   Pareto distribution of cumulative turnover against numbers of customers

If all customers were of exactly the same size in terms of their purchases from the particular supplier, and their cumulative turnover plotted, then the dotted line in Figure 2.1 would result. The further the actual line moves to the left of this straight line the higher the proportion of sales that the top few customers account for. Thus, the steeper the initial ascent of the line, the greater will be the 'concentration' of sales in the hands of a few large customers.

In cases where the top 20 of customers account for about half or more of the total business, it is usually not necessary to continue the cumulative totals thereafter since the tail of the graph can be drawn in approximately with a minimum of error.

Having drawn the Pareto curve, the reader will need to consider several questions.

1   How has this customer distribution come about?
2   Is it the sort of customer concentration that is best for the company?
3   What other customer mixes are possible?
4   What sort of customer distribution is desirable in five or ten years' time?
5   What will be the effect of profitability?

The importance of asking and answering these questions can be seen by looking at an example. Most packaged food companies depend on the multiple grocery outlets for a high proportion of their sales. This has resulted mainly from the advent of super-market shopping which has attracted larger numbers of consumers than the traditional street corner grocery shop. In turn, with the abolition of retail price maintenance, the multiples were able to strengthen their competitive advantage and further increase their bargaining power with their suppliers. What else could the packaged food manufacturers have done but swim with the tide?

Since multiples were accounting for an ever-increasing share of consumers' expenditure on food, a supplier needed to be represented in them or it would lose sales and distribution. In turn the multiples put pressure on their suppliers' margins which led the suppliers to review their cost structure and re-assess the viability of servicing small accounts. Alternative methods were found to perform this function such as use of cash and carry wholesalers. The effect of this was to produce a further concentration of customers.

Contrast this situation with that faced by the tobacco companies. They, like the packaged food companies, saw the trends in retail distribution although RPM was abolished a little later. However, the course of action chosen was different. One major plank in their strategy was to continue to support many thousands of small independent Confectionery, Tobacco and Newsagents shops (CTNs). They also sold to multiples but at prices directly related to the quantity purchased, giving very few if any additional discounts, bonuses or similar concessions. The tobacco companies were able to implement this pricing policy because the large multiples, although accounting for a worthwhile slice of sales, never assumed a dominant position relative to the large volume going through the CTNs. In turn, the effect of their ceasing to trade with any single multiple was not disastrous. Hence the tobacco suppliers were able to impose relatively stringent terms and conditions of trade on their large customers.

Clearly the cost of servicing a large number of CTN accounts is very high for a tobacco company in terms of sales force, distribution, invoicing and credit control costs. However, the cost has proved to be a good investment and has helped the tobacco companies to improve their performance in spite of a contracting market in the UK.

It is not suggested that the fast moving packaged food companies in the first example should or could have followed the same policy but it would be interesting to know (a) how many explicitly asked themselves and answered the *five key questions* set out earlier before determining their customer mix policy, and (b) what alternatives they explored.

2.3 DETERMINING THE BEST CUSTOMER MIX

The starting point for the analysis is a review of company strategy and objectives over the next five or more years. For the purposes of this explanation it will be assumed that the company has a corporate five-year plan which contains the relevant information. If it does not then the information must be obtained from senior management.

The determination of customer mix policy should be tackled in seven steps.

1   Quantify sales objectives for each customer segment for the next five years.
2   Establish number and concentration of customers in each segment.
3   Assess the minimum and maximum number of customers required in each segment to achieve the sales objective.
4   Evaluate the minimum number of customers required for the company as a whole and their Pareto distribution.
5   Evaluate the average total cost of servicing a customer.
6   Assess for every ten additional customers gained the increase in costs and reduction in the company's overall exposure to risk and decide optimum level.
7   Evaluate profit implications and likely variations in customer mix over the next five years, and modify if necessary.

Before looking at each step in more detail it is useful to consider the relevant factors influencing this policy decision. Essentially the main criteria for determining the policy are costs and risks. Any given level of sales can be achieved in one or a combination of these two ways: (a) selling a lot to a few customers, (b) selling a little to many customers.

The fewer the number of customers the greater the risk. If a buyer who takes one fifth of a supplier's turnover decides to use another supplier, then the original supplier will face considerable problems and loss of profit and may even be forced into liquidation. As the numbers of customers increase, the proportion of sales accounted for by the largest few will decrease and hence the risk exposure will decrease also. However, as any operating manager knows, the total cost of servicing increases as the number of customers increases to achieve any given level of sales. The more customers the greater the number of deliveries, salesman calls and invoices, for example. Therefore, costs increase as risk decreases. The best mix of customers will be that which minimises costs at an 'acceptable' level of risk exposure for the company. This lays down the policy which can then provide guidance in making day-to-day decisions.

Two decisions with which senior management are often faced are those of rationalisation and expansion. For example, a supplier might wish to reduce the number of delivery points for its distribution fleet, thus rationalising the number of vehicles and warehouses. To accomplish this requires the transfer of a large number of small customers to distributors who, in turn, increase their proportion of the supplier's business. The wisdom of the decision will be related not only to the savings incurred and any associated reduction in service levels to final customers, which are the factors most often considered, but also to the increase in risk exposure which results. If the resultant customer mix differs markedly from that laid down as company policy then this risk factor should be carefully examined. Similarly, if the supplier is considering expansion into a new market or taking on a major new customer then the resultant greater concentration of customers and hence increased risk must be balanced against the increased sales and profit potential. Often a supplier has no choice. If it wishes to market to the motor manufacturers then a supplier will only have a few large customers. However, once it is apparent that the risks of doing so are large then additional market segments may be explored to reduce overall risk exposure.

Step 1: quantification of sales objectives for each customer segment

Initially it is necessary to carry out a segmentation analysis by customer type. This may be stated in the corporate plan or might need to be deduced from discussions with senior management. The format shown in Table 2.1 shows planned sales turnover for each segment over the next five years. For a grocery company the segments might be multiple retailers, cash and carrys, traditional wholesalers, co-operatives, voluntary groups and department stores. For the capital goods company selling to the electrical power generation industry the segments might be the UK diesel engine manufacturers, the UK gas turbine manufacturers, the UK steam turbine manufacturers, the electrical utilities, the nuclear consortium, contractors and private companies with their own power generation plants.

Table 2.1   Five year sales projections by customer segment

Customer segment	Projected turnover (£million)					Proportion of total sales	
	Next year	Year 2	Year 3	Year 4	Year 5	Next year (%)	Year 5 (%)
1	1.5	1.7	1.8	1.9	1.9	27	13
2	0.5	0.7	1.5	1.9	2.6	9	17
3	1.0	0.9	0.8	0.7	0.6	18	4
4	0.1	0.2	0.4	0.8	1.0	2	7
5	0.4	0.6	0.7	0.9	1.1	7	7
6	1.7	2.4	3.0	3.5	4.0	30	26
7	0.1	0.1	0.2	0.2	0.3	2	2
8	0.1	0.2	0.6	1.2	2.0	2	13
9	0.1	0.1	0.1	0.4	0.6	2	4
10	0.1	0.1	0.2	0.6	1.0	2	7
	5.6	7.0	9.4	12.1	15.1	100	100

Customer segmentation refers to the customers with whom the supplier deals directly, whether distributors or users. As with any form of segmentation analysis, careful consideration is necessary to establish the most useful customer segments.

For the particular supplier used in the example, ten market segments have been identified. Segments 1, 7 and 9 are fairly static over the next five years, segment 3 is declining and segments 2 and 5 are growing fast. The remainder are growing more slowly.

Carrying out this analysis establishes a picture of likely changes in the relative importance in each customer segment over the next five years.

Step 2: establish number and concentration of customers

Next it is necessary to determine the total number and concentration of buying points in each segment. This is shown in Table 2.2 for the particular supplier used in the example in step 1.

Table 2.2   Number of buying points in, concentration of, and size of, each segment

Customer segment	Number of buying points	Proportion of market controlled by top four buying points %	Estimated total purchases next year (£m)
1	80	80	3.5
2	150	40	4.5
3	350	25	1.5
4	20	95	1.0
5	175	80	0.6
6	400	75	2.5
7	40	50	1.0
8	220	15	1.4
9	5	85	0.7
10	9	60	0.6
Total	1,449		

The number of buying points in each segment is shown in the second column. A customer may have one or more buying points depending on where the buying authority is located. A multiple retailer may have several hundred stores each of which places orders on the supplier. However, if, as is common, head office decides which products are authorised and hence can be purchased by the individual outlets, this customer only represents one buying point. If the head office takes away its authorisation and delists the supplier, then no branch can buy and the supplier effectively ceases trading with the multiple. Conversely, if a customer comprises a number of divisions each of which determines its own buying policy autonomously then each division can be regarded as a separate buying point.

The third column shows the buying power concentrated in the hands of the top four buying points in each segment. This gives a good indication of how buying power is distributed. It is of interest to note, for example, that although segment 6, which is one of the supplier's major growth areas, has 400 customers, three-quarters of the segment is controlled by only four customers.

The final column shows the estimated total purchases for each segment projected for the following year. Comparison with Table 2.1 enables desired market share in each segment to be evaluated for next year, which should act as a further check on the realism of the sales forecasts made. A variety of sources will need to be used to obtain the necessary information to complete the third and final columns including desk research, market surveys and feedback from sales staff.

Step 3: establish required minimum and maximum customer number

Next it is necessary to calculate the minimum and maximum number of buying points in each segment which are required to achieve the sales objectives. This is done in the following way, taking segment 1 as an example. The top four buying points control 80 per cent of the market or £2.8 million of purchases (80 per cent of £3.5 million). The objective for next year is £1.5 million. This can be achieved in a number of ways determined by the Pareto distribution of purchasing power. Figure 2.2 shows the Pareto curve for segment 1.

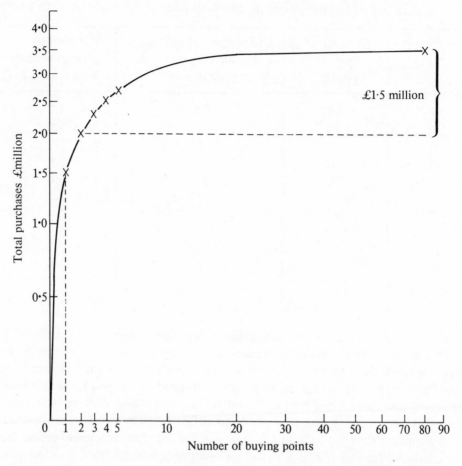

Figure 2.2   Pareto distribution of purchasing power in segment 1

The curve shows that the minimum number of buying points required is 1, i.e. the largest one in that segment, and it is necessary to obtain 100 per cent of his business to achieve the sales objective of £1.5 million. The maximum number of customers is 80 although unless the largest and second largest customers are included it is not possible to achieve the sales target with fewer than 78 customers (i.e. 80 – 2), and it is necessary to get all the business these 78 customers have to offer. It may be concluded that such a situation is unlikely and that some business will need to be obtained from the two large customers to meet the sales target.

In determining the minimum number of customers a view must be taken of the proportion of the business that will be obtained from each of the larger customers. For example, in segment 2 the top four buying points account for £1.8 million (Table 2.2: 40 per cent × £4.5 million) of sales. If the largest customer buys, say, £0.7 million then the sales objective of £0.5m could theoretically be achieved through one customer. However, if the customer's purchasing policy is such that the supplier can realistically only hope to obtain 25 per cent of his purchases then additional customers must be sought. On this basis the supplier estimates that a minimum of five customers are required to achieve the sales objective for next year.

A similar exercise should be carried out for the other segments. Thus, for each segment a picture of all the alternatives will emerge, showing the minimum and maximum number of buying points and the possible variations which will enable the sales objective to be achieved for next year. This is summarised in Table 2.3.

Table 2.3 Minimum and maximum number of buying points

Segment	Minimum number of buying points	Maximum number of buying points
1	1	80
2	5	150
3	30	350
4	3	20
5	14	175
6	19	400
7	2	40
8	6	220
9	6	5
10	4	9
Total	90	1,449

Step 4: draw the Pareto distribution for the minimum number of customers

From Table 2.3 it is apparent that the minimum number of buying points needed to meet the company sales objectives is 90 and the maximum nearly 1,450. The corresponding curve should be drawn and Figure 2.3 presents the picture for the minimum number of 90 buying points. This is completed by listing all the customers in decreasing order of sales and shows, for the whole company, the greatest possible concentration of customers and hence the maximum level of risk exposure.

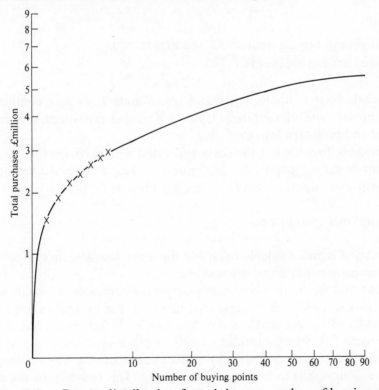

Figure 2.3   Pareto distribution for minimum number of buying points

Step 5: evaluate average total servicing cost per customer

It is now necessary to look at the costs associated with servicing individual buying points. In particular, those costs which are likely to vary as the number of customers increases from 90 to 1,449. The following categories of cost are relevant: (a) sales costs, (b) warehousing costs, (c) distribution costs, (d) order processing costs, (e) invoicing costs.

The precise way in which these costs vary will be unique to each company. It may be that a new warehouse is required at some point or more office space must be built. In deciding which costs are relevant a choice exists between taking marginal costs or average cost. The appropriate choice will depend upon the individual circumstances. The higher the ratio of direct to total costs the more valid will be average cost figures. The lower the ratio of direct to total costs the less valid will be the average cost figures and attempts should be made to measure the marginal costs, i.e. the incremental cost incurred for each additional customer serviced. For the purposes of the example and the sake of simplicity, it is assumed that average costs provide a reasonable guide to the likely movement of costs with increasing number of customers.

The average costs are calculated in the following way. First, all fixed, semi-fixed and variable costs associated with each function are identified, i.e. the total cost. This is divided by the number of actual buying points to obtain the average cost.

Total costs	£m
Sales	0.5
Warehousing	0.9
Distribution	0.7
Order processing	0.2
Invoicing	0.1
Total costs	£2.4

Actual number of buying points 735 (see Figure 2.1)
Average cost per buying point £3,625

The latest realistic figures should be used. Where a budget has been compiled for next year this will provide the relevant data. If no such budget exists then this year's figures should be used and projected into next year.

It is now possible to work out the costs associated with servicing the possible spread of buying point as shown graphically in Figure 2.4. This enables the total cost of supplying any number of buying points to be quickly obtained.

Step 6: assess optimal customer mix

All the information is now available to enable the most desirable mix of accounts to be decided and company policy to be established.

It is apparent that as the number of buying points decreases, an increasing proportion of total sales will go to the largest customers. In the example shown the biggest customer accounts for 27 per cent and the top seven for 54 per cent of business next year as shown in Figure 2.3. When a similar analysis is conducted for year 5 it is seen that this picture does not change dramatically in five years' time when the proportion for the top seven accounts falls to just under 50 per cent. This clearly puts the company at risk. If any major account is lost then the impact on the company will be highly

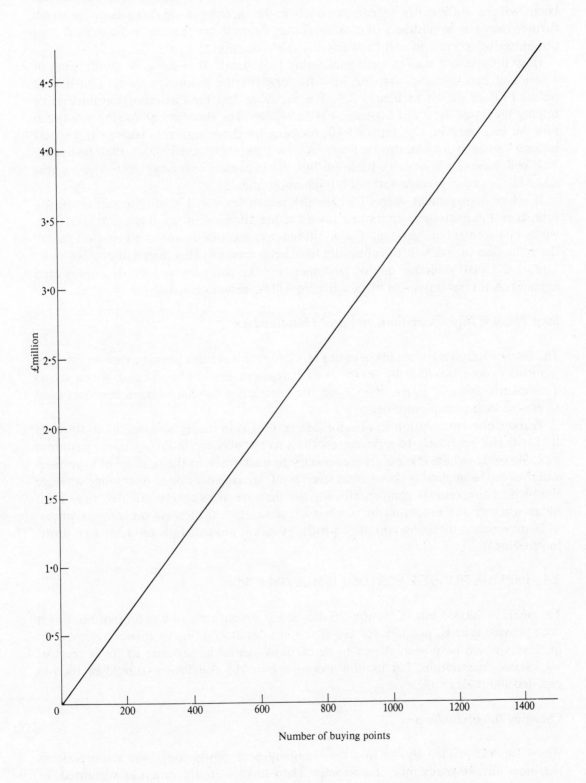

Figure 2.4   Total servicing costs

detrimental. As the number of buying points increases, the risk decreases, but the servicing costs increase.

Clearly, there will be a point where senior management considers that the risk has been reduced sufficiently to compensate for the increase in servicing cost. Although further increases in numbers of customers may be perfectly feasible, management does not judge the increase in cost to justify the risk reduction.

How does senior management make this judgement? It is done by the drawing of a series of Pareto curves starting with the one for the minimum number of buying points (90) as shown in Figure 2.3. The servicing cost for this minimum number of buying points as shown in Figure 2.4 is £294,000. The numbers of buying points can now be increased in, say, units of 10, focusing on those segments where the greatest impact on risk reduction can be made. A new Pareto distribution can then be drawn. This will present a lower risk situation but the increase in servicing costs will be over £32,650 (i.e. 10 × average cost per buying point £3,625).

If senior management judges that the risk reduction is well worth the extra expenditure, then the exercise is continued for a further addition of ten buying points. Only when management judges that the additional expenditure is not compensated for by the reduction in risk will the optimum have been reached. This then will provide a picture of the most desirable mix of customers for the company as a whole and for each segment. A formal statement of this picture will represent company policy.

Step 7: assess future variations and profit implications

The likely future variations in customer mix over the next five years in view of the long term sales objectives and the trends in each segment need to be assessed. If this shows a substantial increase in risk then it may be necessary to compromise in the short term to get the long term picture right.

Throughout, no mention has been made of profit. In nearly all cases it will turn out that it is still profitable to service even the smallest account in the optimum customer mix. However, where it is not, it is necessary to back-track to the number of customers where even the smallest is above break-even level. Management must now judge whether the profit improvement compensates for the increase in risk. In particular, they must judge whether the reduction in number of accounts will increase pressure on prices. This may occur to the extent that profit levels are eroded, thus reducing any profit improvement.

2.4 IMPLICATIONS OF CUSTOMER MIX POLICY

The analysis carried out in section 2.3 has many simplifications and limitations, but it does provide a basis, possibly for the first time, for attempting to answer a number of questions which have been shown to be of fundamental importance to the success of a business organisation. Let us now examine how the conclusions should be used in practice and their implications.

Changing the customer mix

Where the analysis has shown that the company is currently some way removed from the most advantageous mix of customers then further consideration is warranted. In particular, if there is a need to increase the number of customers in some of the segments then certain specific questions must be answered.

1   How many new customers are required?
2   Who are they likely to be?
3   What is it likely to cost to get them?
4   How long will it take?
5   What will be the effect on existing customers and how will they react?

The most difficult question to answer is the last where there are a number of judge-mental factors to be considered. Where a particular agreement exists between the supplier and a distributor, giving the latter a geographic territory franchise, then the appointment of competing distributors will be problematical. Even where no such formal agreement exists such actions may be very difficult to take. A case in point is a large supplier of components to the automotive spare parts market which has over 80 per cent of its sales with four distributors. It did not have to carry out the analysis in section 2.3 to know it needed to increase the number of distributors (although if it had done so at an earlier stage, it may never have got into its present situation). But how could it do so without putting a substantial proportion of its business at risk by driving an existing distributor to a competitive supplier?

A number of possibilities are open including buying a large distributor, by-passing the distributors and going direct to the user or tackling the problem on a region-by-region or segment-by-segment basis. Each has distinct disadvantages. Thus, there is often a risk involved for the company in trying to reduce its risk exposure. Whether to take the risk is a judgement decision based on the facts determined in the preceding section. The benefit of the analysis is that it will quantify the implications of the deci-sion to be made. It will do so in three ways. The extra costs of servicing the additional distributors will be evaluated. The overall reduction in the company's risk exposure will be identified. The specific risks associated with alienating existing distributors can be assessed. If the additional risk plus costs incurred is more than compensated for by the overall reduction in company risk exposure then new distributors should be ap-pointed. If not then no action should be taken.

Current mix of customers is optimal

Where the analysis shows that the present customer mix is more or less optimal then the company has every reason to be satisfied, but not complacent. In particular, it is vital that the current situation be projected into the future to see if it is likely to change to the detriment of the supplier.

The supplier's management may face internal pressures, particularly during inflation-ary times, for cost reduction. Suggestions may be made to reduce the servicing of small customers since analysis may have shown these to be less profitable. The onus on the marketing man must be to relate the resultant loss of customers to the optimal cus-tomer mix desired, to judge whether the actual cost-saving and associated smaller revenue loss will outweigh the present and possible future increase in risk.

Subjective factors

Whenever a supplier is considering changing its customer mix, particularly when it is determining whether to reduce its servicing levels, there is likely to be some resistance internally to the change. This will tend to be most strong amongst the sales force for obvious reasons such as (a) loss of sales turnover, (b) discarding customers who have been loyal, (c) giving the company a bad reputation. Although the tangible impact of these may be small the motivational impact on the sales force can be significant. It is therefore important, when deciding to change the customer mix, to communicate effectively with the sales force, giving the reasons and benefits behind this policy.

The nature of risk

It has been assumed that the fewer customers a supplier has the more exposed to risk he becomes. Let us examine in more detail why this should be so, taking first the most extreme situation.

If a supplier only has one customer then he is totally dependent on this customer for his prosperity. His sales, distribution, administration costs, etc., will be correspondingly low. What risks does the supplier face? A significant one is that the customer will become bankrupt. Another important risk is that the customer will go to a competitive supplier and cease trading with the original supplier. Fortunately, this rarely occurs without considerable prior warning.

One policy that is sometimes suggested is that the supplier should in turn make the customer as heavily dependent on him as possible. This will tend to increase the likelihood of the customer integrating his operation further and acquiring a part or total stake in the supplier. If this is the supplier's objective then it is clearly a sensible policy to follow, but if he wishes to continue in business independently it does very little to reduce his risk.

For his part the major customer is very unlikely to allow himself to get into a sole supplier position, although in some situations the big buyer may be forced to buy from one supplier because of the particular technology or patents involved. However, the buyer will generally seek to decrease his dependence on a single supplier. Typically, for example, the car manufacturers will nearly always dual source their supplies where possible.

The main risk with a large customer, however, is that he will exert his power to the detriment of the supplier. In particular, the customer rather than the supplier may seek to determine price, quality and delivery, for example. It is not in the customer's interest to drive his supplier out of business by forcing prices too low or demanding too much service, but the buyer must strive to maximise the overall benefit for his own company. Thus, although the supplier will survive with probably an adequate return on capital, he loses freedom of action. This in turn reduces the possibility of the supplier earning a considerably higher return which would come about if he could 'trim his sales' to suit the direction he, rather than his customer, would wish to go.

A further dimension of risk is related to the particular segment(s) in which the supplier chooses to operate. For example, subcontractors or component suppliers to individual industries such as ship builders and car manufacturers are notoriously vulnerable to the business cycles in these industries. The decision to spread the risk over a larger number of industries is a function of overall marketing strategy, and not one of customer mix policy.

2.5 SUMMARY

This chapter looked at a method which can be used by a supplier to determine the best mix of customers, commensurate with the risk that the supplier is willing to accept to achieve its long term objectives. This involves a seven step procedure which enables company policy to be formulated.

The desirability of carrying out this analysis will vary from company to company. However, even in the situation where the supplier is perfectly aware of what needs to be done to reduce his risk, and his main concern is how to do it, the analysis is useful since it will help the supplier to avoid getting into the same situation again.

The practical implications of the analysis have been discussed and a further guide given to enable management to reach the best decisions on its customer mix policy. The implications of this policy determination for the senior manager are that he can set objectives for the numbers of accounts which must be opened or closed in each segment, having first established the resultant total impact on the business. This in turn, is a key in determining the most suitable organisation structure.

Action planning checklist

Questions	Answers and action	Timing of action and evaluation
1 What is the Pareto distribution curve of my present customer mix?		
2 In what way, if any, would I wish this mix to change?		
3 Projecting current trends and relating these to company objectives, how will the Pareto curve look in five and ten years' time?		
4 Is this where I would wish to be or should action be taken to change the customer mix?		

3
Structuring the organisation

3.1 INTRODUCTION

Organisation structures are essentially a compromise between the market's needs, the company's objectives and the functional responsibilities of company departments. Many companies are unable to maximise the return they get from major customers because their organisation structure is not geared to the job to be done. In particular, the responsibility for selling is often held at too low a level while the logistical support that needs to be given to sales is inadequate. Such was the case with an office machinery and supplies company where the national accounts department was of insufficient status and authority to ensure that delivery and service to its customers matched their requirements.

The appropriate structure varies from company to company and market to market. Grocery companies typically have key account executives selling to and negotiating with the large multiples, assisted by product or brand managers who also visit the big buyers. In some instances, these departments have developed further to the extent that all the large account sales personnel and associated marketing and support staff are now in one department, headed by a general manager. Similar situations exist in companies marketing industrial products. One industrial company has created a special department, headed by a marketing manager, dealing solely with the British Steel Corporation, separating it from its general engineering business.

Increasingly, companies are structuring not only their field organisations, but also their internal sales administration, in order to allocate specific responsibility to them for handling major customers. Many steel stockholders, for example, have teamed their internal desk sales staff with their outside salesmen around key customers. Another industrial company's approach is to recruit a sales engineer with management potential to develop a particular market segment. Then, as the sales to that segment increase, a separate production section is established and the sales engineer is promoted to general management responsible for the segment.

Unfortunately, many companies find these organisation changes difficult to implement because some managers and sales staff will have their responsibilities increased whilst those of others will be decreased. In addition they fail to consider the salary implications of the new structure. One snack food manufacturer, for example, formed a national accounts department to service the head offices of the retail multiples which is a common structure in the consumer goods industry. This new department was established separately from its large field sales force which had traditionally looked after these major customers. However the resentment from the senior sales managers, resulting in poor implementation, was so strong that after less than two years the new department was disbanded and the function reintegrated with the field sales activity. In effect the new department had been isolated and as a result became increasingly ineffective.

This chapter looks at the main points that the senior manager should consider in assessing his current organisation structure and relating this structure to the needs of his large customers. It then discusses the nature and scale of changes that might be necessary. The experienced manager will know that many forms of organisation structure can be made to function. Even where the formal lines of communication and organisation structure may inhibit efficient working, informal lines are developed by the personnel involved to facilitate the task to be carried out. This process will, however, generally be inefficient in the sense that there is likely to be a duplication of effort, unequal allocation of work, lack of clear responsibilities, multiple reporting relationships, complex systems and so on. All these factors militate against the smooth functioning of the organisation and mean that the staff spend excessive amounts of time trying to overcome these difficulties, rather than tackling the job in hand. In turn the service received by the customer can be severely affected. Where this customer is a large one, the effect on the company can indeed be serious. Thus in developing his organisation structure to handle major customers the managing or marketing director will often have a choice amongst a number of alternatives, all of which will work, but some will work better than others.

3.2   CRITERIA FOR AN EFFECTIVE ORGANISATION STRUCTURE

The decision on the most suitable organisation structure to handle major customers is both complex and individual to each company. It cannot be considered in isolation but must be related to the total structure required to deal effectively with all customers both large and small. The most suitable structure must be designed to enable the overall company policy (as defined in Chapter 2) to be implemented. If there is a need to open up many new large customers, the structure is likely to be different from that required merely to defend the current position in existing customers.

In addition the organisation structure should take into account six further factors:

  (a)   the market;
  (b)   the task to be carried out;
  (c)   minimum overlap of activity;
  (d)   clear job specifications;
  (e)   ease of communication;
  (f)   the concept of commitment.

The market

The organisation structure should be market oriented and flexible enough to cope with change. Thus, the structure must reflect the needs of the customers and the way in which these and company needs change. For example, if a supplier is structured on a divisional basis, each division selling different products to the same customer and possibly even the same buyer, then it is likely the customer's needs will be better served by only one salesman visiting the buyer, rather than many. In addition it will be less difficult for the supplier to co-ordinate the various divisional offerings so that they represent a coherent package to the customer. Further, the co-ordination of the supplier's sales and distribution effort is made easier. Even where the product offerings are of a highly technical nature, requiring a different sales engineer to sell each one, it will still be advantageous to co-ordinate the total sales activity to individual major customers.

In another market the supplier may be dealing with multinational customers. The appropriate structure must take into account the authority of head office over the individual operating units in each country and the relative autonomy of the latter. Language and cultural differences between countries must also be considered.

The degree to which the supplier responds to these differences in customer structure depends on the importance of the customer as determined by company policy. Clearly the more important the customer, the more necessary an explicit organisational response.

Task to be carried out

All necessary duties to achieve the sales objective must be covered. For example, a company selling building products to the construction industry must contact the customer's buying department, enter into price negotiations, give technical advice and support, provide samples and trials, and give assistance in specification to achieve its objectives. This activity must be carried out with the commercial and technical staff of building companies, architects, local authorities and government departments.

Therefore, the organisation structure must be geared to ensure that all these sales, marketing and sales support functions can be carried out effectively. The scale of this activity is likely to be greater and more complex with major customers than with minor ones. In turn this will reflect on the resources the supplier must bring to bear.

Minimum overlap of activity

No duplication of effort should be necessary. Overlapping calling and more than one person carrying out the same task with each customer should be avoided if possible. Thus, for example, two individuals negotiating promotions for two different product lines from the same supplier with a national multiple grocery chain would indicate a duplication of effort. Similarly, two applications engineers visiting the same customer to discuss similar problems would indicate a less than optimal efficiency.

Overlapping activity is only occasionally a problem with smaller customers since there will be relatively few contacts. With major customers, since more staff will normally be involved, it increases in importance.

Clear job specifications

Everyone must understand clearly the limits of his responsibility and authority, what his job is, and how it fits into the whole structure. This requires the compilation of a job description and in particular a definition of how the job affects the total service received by the customer and hence his satisfaction with the supplier. Used correctly clear job descriptions will greatly help the effective working and control of the organisation. Unfortunately, if badly used they will constrain activity and hinder smooth operation.

The key factors are to ensure that the job descriptions are introduced intelligently so as to elicit the greatest amount of commitment from the staff concerned and that they are subsequently used to *help* individuals rather than to allocate blame. Both these tasks are difficult and require careful planning.

Ease of communication

Since the servicing of major accounts generally involves members from different functions within the company it is important that mechanisms exist to enable information to flow easily between them. This means communication must flow horizontally across functions as well as vertically to and through line management.

Concept of commitment

Traditionally salesmen have been charged with the responsibility of achieving a given amount of sales revenue from a geographic sales territory. This has covered both large and small customers and, generally, sales management was not concerned with which customers produced the sales as long as the total sales target was achieved. The salesman thus had a commitment to his territory.

The increasing importance of major customers has caused suppliers to introduce this concept of commitment with commensurate responsibility to individual large customers. The salesman and the relevant support personnel will therefore be judged on the effectiveness with which they handle, and the results produced from, major accounts. Thus, if the company is seeking to increase the effectiveness with which it handles major accounts it must generally increase the commitment towards them. The nature and scale of this commitment is discussed below.

3.3   ORGANISING FOR MAJOR CUSTOMERS

The nature of the organisation structure needed to service the requirements of major customers depends on company policy and should aim to satisfy the criteria discussed in section 2.3. To determine the most suitable structure it is necessary to answer the following four questions.

1   What is the task that needs to be carried out to obtain business from major customers?
2   How many staff, of what type, are needed?
3   How should their efforts be co-ordinated?
4   Who is responsible for major customers?

Each of these questions will be examined in detail.

Task to be carried out

To establish the tasks to be carried out it is necessary to conduct research and analysis of the buying systems, identifying the level and variety of influencers, decision makers, buyers and users. In addition, the number and variety of locations within the major customers must also be determined. This will enable the supplier to list the tasks he needs to carry out to achieve his objectives for the particular type of account. Tables 3.1 and 3.2 show the summary results of such an analysis for a consumer goods company and a building products supplier. These two customer service analyses present an overall picture of the nature and scale of the task to be carried out for each major customer type.

The next step is to identify the knowledge, skill and authority required from the individuals who are carrying out the task. In effect this requires a fuller examination of each of the 'tasks to be carried out' and the identification within the current organisation structure of the personnel who currently carry out the various functions. Table 3.3 shows how this is done for the first type of account, national building companies, to be serviced by the building products supplier shown in Table 3.2.

Having completed this analysis, it is now possible to begin to identify whether the activities can be regrouped amongst the individuals concerned so as to *increase* the *commitment* to that segment of customers in line with the defined company policy.

Table 3.1   Customer service requirement analysis: consumer goods (food)

Type of account	Number of accounts	Tasks to be carried out
1 National multiples (a) Head offices	20	Contract purchasing Price negotiation Own brand deals National promotions
(b) Branches	1,000	Local ordering Merchandising
2 Co-operative societies (a) Head offices	10	Contract purchasing Price negotiation Own brand deals Promotions
(b) Branches	500	Merchandising
3 Voluntary groups (a) Head offices	6	Contract purchasing Price negotiation Own brand deals Promotions
(b) Branches	5,000	Nil
4 Regional multiples (a) Head offices	50	Purchasing Regional promotions
(b) Branches	200	Local merchandising
5 Independent stores	5,000	Purchasing Account collection

Table 3.2   Customer service requirement analysis: industrial goods (building products)

Type of account	Number of accounts	Tasks to be carried out
National building companies	20	Purchasing Price negotiation Technical advice Samples and trials Long term planning
Local building companies	1,000	Purchasing Technical support
Architects	500	Technical advice Assistance in specifying
Local authorities	300	Technical advice Assistance in specifying
Government departments	20	Purchasing Technical advice
Property developers	40	Technical advice Marketing advice

Table 3.3   Detailed customer service requirement analysis:
industrial goods (sales to national building companies)

Type of account	Tasks	Details	Personnel responsible
National building companies	Purchasing	Regular visits to chief buyer and product buyer.	Sales managers and sales representatives
		Discussions on new products and existing contracts.	Technical representatives Contracts manager
		Discussions on possible future contracts.	Sales representatives
		Identification and resolution of administrative, quality and delivery problems.	Sales representatives Contracts manager Technical manager Office manager Distribution manager
		Notification and issue of specific quotations required.	Sales representatives Quotations clerks
		Writing visit reports with action copies to internal staff as necessary.	Sales representatives Quotations clerks
	Price negotiation	Establishing pricing policy.	Marketing director
		Setting price level on individual quotations.	Office manager Quotations clerks
		Negotiating with buyer below quoted price.	Sales managers
	Technical advice	Provision of technical specifications.	Technical manager
		Assistance to quantity surveyors; drawing office staff, architects, design engineers and civil engineers on properties and usage of products.	Technical representatives Sales representatives
		Advice to site management on product application.	Applications specialists
	Samples and trials	Obtaining samples of materials (base materials, etc.) on which products to be used.	Sales representatives
		Testing products in difficult environmental conditions.	Technical manager Laboratory staff
		Examining product complaints.	Laboratory staff
	Long term planning	Discussions on current service offered and future relationships with senior customer personnel.	Marketing director

The analysis shows that there are a large number of individuals involved with servicing national building companies, ranging from the marketing director to the sales office clerks. Clearly it may be possible to reallocate this activity so that it takes up a larger proportion of the available time of a few personnel, rather than a little time of a lot of people, thus increasing their commitment.

Further, if overall policy has indicated a need to substantially increase sales within existing national building companies and also the desirability of substantially increasing the numbers of accounts of this size, then the reorganisation of activity shown in Figure 3.1 would prove advantageous.

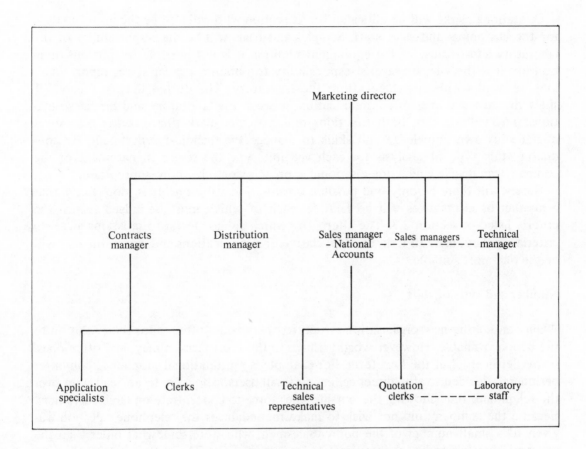

Figure 3.1   Organisation structure: industrial goods (sales to national building companies)

This new organisation involves the appointment of a 'sales manager – national accounts', responsible for sales and service to the national building companies. The sales manager will have the authority to negotiate price up to a fixed limit off-standard price although he will be judged on the profit of the business his section obtains. Reporting to him will be technical sales representatives, a new function, who will be responsible for selling, handling technical matters and liaison with the customer on a day to day basis. These customers should be grouped on the basis of the type of building they carry out, e.g. office development, speculative private housing, local authority housing, civil engineering, construction, factories, and the technical sales representatives organised accordingly. Although most of the large construction companies will operate across a number of different building categories, they will tend to structure their organisation to separate their approach to each. In addition the types of influencers associated with each will differ, i.e. architects, surveyors, civil engineers, local authority personnel, developers. Furthermore, the technical problems associated with the application of the suppliers' products in each type of construction will vary. Therefore it is sensible for each technical sales representative to specialise in a similar fashion. This will involve more than one supplier's salesman visiting each customer, but, since they will probably be visiting different locations and contacts, little duplication of calling will take place. However, as compared with the traditional structure of geographic territory based salesmen, distances travelled and salesmen's expenses will increase and call rate may decrease, but often this will be more than compensated for by the improved results achieved.

Quotations clerks will be allocated to the section who will also be the inside contact for the customers and sales staff. Samples and trials will be the responsibility of the laboratory and because of the equipment required it is not possible to split this function but it is the sales manager's responsibility to obtain a regular status report on all jobs, relevant to his customers, from the laboratory. The dotted lines in Figure 3.1 show the informal lines of communication between the laboratory and the sales functions. To facilitate this, both functions report to the marketing director, who must upgrade his own knowledge and skills to manage the technical department. By conducting this type of analysis for each account type the senior management of the company can decide which organisational approach would be more appropriate.

Rarely will there be only one possible organisation structure. It is more likely that a number of alternatives will be feasible, each of which must be judged against the criteria listed in section 2.3. The alternative which comes closest to satisfying all seven criteria – policy, market, task, overlap, clarity, communications and commitment – will be the one most suitable.

Number and type of staff

When considering new organisation structures, companies often tailor their solution to the people available. However worthy this is in the short term, it may, and often does, prove detrimental in the long term. For example, a multinational supplier of computer peripherals decided to stop direct calling on small users, who were to be dealt with over the telephone, thus allowing the outside sales force to concentrate on large customers. Because the company did not wish to make redundancies the telephone sales job was given to a small number of the poorer salesmen, who were somewhat older than the rest and were felt to be inappropriate to large customers. The net result was that the new telephone sales activity was unable to contact the many smaller accounts as frequently as required because the salesmen had not been trained in telephone techniques and how to organise their time, and they felt aggrieved since they were not able to utilise their face to face sales skills over the telephone and were therefore losing business.

The outside sales force appeared to be much more successful since each salesman had fewer, large accounts and was able to devote more time to each one and obtain more business. But the question of whether the same results could have been achieved with fewer salesmen was not asked, the reason being that all the salesmen appeared to be very busy and sales were increasing. Such growth situations often hide a large number of problems which frequently do not come to the surface until the growth rate eases off. Unfortunately it is often too late by then and much disruption will be caused in remedying the situation.

To ensure that staffing levels are commensurate with the task to be carried out a workload analysis should be undertaken. The aim is to build the organisation from the bottom upwards, thereby giving the appropriate level of service to each customer and the appropriate amount of work to each man. This in turn will enable the number of management levels to be determined.

The common factor between individuals doing different jobs is the number of working hours they have available and this should be the starting point for such a workload analysis. The amount of work per individual can then be evaluated by assessing the elements of the sales job.

If a sophisticated approach is needed, work study methods or activity sampling, for example, can be used. However, for most practical purposes it is sufficient to estimate, from experience, the time taken to carry out the various tasks. This can be cross checked by discussions with those currently carrying out the tasks. Taking the quotations clerks as an example, the major tasks to be carried out should be linked together with the time taken to carry them out as shown in Table 3.4. The number of staff required can then be calculated.

Table 3.4   Time required to carry out clerical tasks

	Activity	Time
1	Preparing quotations	1 day per quotation
2	Customer telephone discussions	½ hour per customer
3	Liaison with laboratory	1 hour per job per week
4	Liaison with contracts manager	1 hour per job per week
5	Analysing sales reports	1 day per week for whole department
6	Attending department meetings	½ day per week per man
7	Personal administration	2 hours per week per man
8	Lunch	1 hour per day per man

It will be noted that the total time spent on some activities, such as telephone discussions, depends on the number of customers, whilst others, such as analysing sales reports, require a fixed amount of time, irrespective of the number of customers.

The next step is to convert the activity/time relationships into a purely time one enabling the staffing level to be worked out, as in Table 3.5. To make this calculation certain extra information is required and this is shown at the top of the illustration.

The number of quotations clerks required as shown in Table 3.5 is three, rounded up from the exact number which is 2.84. However, if the answer had come to 2.3 or less, management might have considered rounding down to two clerks, expecting the additional workload to be absorbed.

Staffing levels are therefore calculated using the following formula:

$$\frac{\text{Total number of working days required per year}}{\text{Number of working days available per man per year}}$$

When carrying out such calculations, it is not uncommon to identify positions where it is not possible for an individual section or department to generate sufficient workload to keep an individual fully occupied. For example, each sales section in the building materials supply company used in the example might require the services of two-thirds of an applications specialist, who provides advice to the customer after he has bought the product. If there are five sales sections, then in reaching his decision on the appropriate level of staffing the senior manager has a number of options.

1   Each section has one applications specialist, his spare time being utilised to resolve other technical problems, i.e. redefining the workload.

2   A central resource will be established with three applications specialists reporting to the contracts manager working for all five departments (as shown in Figure 3.1).

3   A combination of the two.

Table 3.5   Calculating staffing levels

Number of actual and potential customers: 20
Average number of quotation requests per year per customer: 10
Average number of jobs being undertaken at any one time: 12
Working week: 40 hours with 1 hour lunch per day

Total number of clerical working days required per year

1	Preparing quotations	$1 \times 10 \times 20$	= 200
2	Customer telephone discussion	$\frac{1}{2} \times \frac{1}{8} \times 52 \times 20$	= 65
3	Laboratory liaison	$\frac{1}{8} \times 12 \times 52$	= 78
4	Contract liaison	$\frac{1}{8} \times 12 \times 52$	= 78
5	Analysis of sales reports	1×52	= 52
		Total annual working days	= 473

Number of working days available per man per year

Total days per year		365
Less Weekends	104	
Holidays	20	
Sickness	5	
Training	5	
Department meetings ($\frac{1}{2} \times 46$) =	23	
Personal admin ($\frac{1}{4} \times 46$) =	11½	
Lunch ($\frac{1}{8} \times 5 \times 46$)=	28¾	
Conferences	1½	198¾
Number of working days		166¼

Number of quotations clerks required $\dfrac{473}{166\frac{1}{4}}$ = 3 approximately

Note: 20 days' holiday, 5 days' sickness and 5 days' training reduce the working year to $52 - 4 - 1 - 1 = 46$ weeks. The department meetings, etc., only occur during these working weeks.

The choice as to which type of structure is more appropriate will depend upon the following.

1   The degree of technical expertise and knowledge needed for each application and the likelihood of one individual being able to know sufficient about two or more applications to carry out the job effectively.
2   The level of commitment required from the application engineer to achieve the sales objectives for individual section.
3   The amount of overlap of application between the various sections.
4   The likely future changes in workload levels.

Co-ordinating the staff

In a traditional organisation the salesman does the selling, the sales office the sales administration, the marketing department the advertising, promotions and marketing planning, the distribution department the distribution and so on. The effective servicing of major accounts, however, as previously discussed, requires considerable overlap and co-operation between the various specialist functions. In effect the various functions are grouped together to provide the best service to the customer. The nature of this grouping will vary from company to company but the need to co-ordinate the specialist activities more extensively than ever before will remain the same.

The line reporting relationships and the nature and flow of the day to day workload can either facilitate or impede the effective working of the total effort to major accounts. In organising the workflow, therefore, it is essential to look at both the way each individual organises his work and how this interrelates with the other functions. The situation where one function optimises its own operations to the detriment of the whole should be avoided. For example, an outside major account salesman, in the desire to make the optimum use of his time, may divide his territory into various segments using a 'petal' system to cover his calls and minimise his travel distance. If by so doing he fails to follow up an urgent outstanding enquiry, or does not resolve an important technical problem, or obtains orders which distribution will have difficulty in coping with, or arrives shortly after his contact has spoken to the internal quotations clerk, his very 'efficiency' will cause strains on the organisation and lead to a reduction of effective customer service.

To reduce the possibility of this occurring requires a close examination of the interaction between the various functions. The activities required to obtain business from the major account should be split up in a manner similar to that shown in Table 3.3. All the personnel involved with the activity (in the redefined structure) should be listed together with the workflow between them, at least for the most important activities. This will help to overcome problems such as the salesman expecting the quotations clerk to check the status of all his outstanding quotations by telephoning customers on Friday morning when, at that time, the clerk expects to be discussing the following week's delivery schedules with the distribution manager.

In a dynamic situation such an analysis, although initially very worthwhile, will quickly become out of date. Communication mechanisms and control systems need to be established to overcome these problems as they arise. One method of doing this is by holding regular meetings with the relevant staff. When all the personnel concerned are in one department this is generally fairly straightforward. However, when there is a spread of reporting relationships the likelihood of a meeting between, say, the distribution manager, the quotations clerk, sales manager and research manager is greatly reduced. The possibility of continuing such meetings with the necessary frequency is not very great. For one thing the customers concerned may only take up a relatively small part of the time of the various functional heads.

Thus, regular meetings are unlikely to be held unless all functions are incorporated under one line manager. The solution lies in the individuals who have the greatest commitment to the customer group influencing those who have a lesser commitment to be aware of the problem and its implications. This is not dissimilar to the role of the product or brand manager who has total responsibility for his products but no authority over production, sales force and distribution, for example. His success, as with that of the good major accounts manager, depends on how effectively he can influence other functions to cater for the needs of that part of the business for which he is directly responsible. That this requires knowledge and interpersonal skills somewhat beyond that of the pure sales function is overlooked by many companies. The implications for the quality of staff required, their remuneration system and the training they need are vitally important.

Responsibility for major customers

The nature of the major accounts organisation indicates that managerially it often represents a complex problem. Where all the staff are in one department then the normal consideration of spans of control and workload analysis, for example, are relevant. However, as previously discussed, this is usually the exception rather than the rule. Normally the line management concerned will be function-oriented rather than major customer-oriented because their first commitment is to operating an efficient factory, distribution operation, research laboratory and marketing department, rather than satisfying the needs of a few major customers.

The effect of this on the communication and co-ordination process has been discussed in the preceding section but the question arises of who, if anyone, is responsible and accountable for major customers. Traditionally, even where there has been a major account salesman, or sales manager, no one except possibly the managing director or marketing director has been specifically responsible for all aspects of selling to and servicing major accounts. The salesman has been responsible for selling, but no one has been responsible for profit. In particular, no one has had responsibility for organising and directing the company's resources towards large customers so as to maximise the return obtained from them.

Increasingly, however, companies are finding it necessary to reorient themselves towards the concept of giving individuals responsibility for major accounts and, in particular, the profit achieved from them. Frequently the individual charged with this responsibility will be the salesman concerned. To carry out this task effectively requires not only a considerable upgrading in knowledge and skills but also a change in perception by the salesman of his role and also by the rest of the organisation. Such a change is often difficult to bring about and in companies where it does not occur the supplier is missing a good opportunity to increase his performance and profitability.

3.4 EXAMPLES OF ORGANISATION STRUCTURES

The preceding sections have shown how a company should set about developing the most suitable organisation structure to handle major customers. This approach is only a specific application of the general method that should be used when senior management is considering organisation changes and it is clear that the question of the most suitable structure for major customers cannot be considered in isolation from the rest of the organisation structure. For example, if additional resources and attention are focused on large customers, then it is likely that less attention will be paid to smaller ones. The impact of both types of customer must be assessed.

In practice, suppliers have adopted a variety of different organisational responses to the challenge of major customers. Some of the more usual will be discussed in detail.

Special accounts salesman

This type of structure is the simplest organisational response that a supplier can make.

It is sometimes a precursor to the national accounts department described in the next section, and occurs across all types of industries. Typically, as shown in Figure 3.2, the sales activity in each area is divided between a few special accounts salesmen and a larger number of area representatives, all of whom report to the first line sales manager. The special accounts salesmen will concentrate on the larger customers and cover a number of area salesmen's territories. These accounts will not generally be called on by the area salesman. In many instances, particularly in industrial and service markets, the major customers will have needs for particular products or applications. Thus, the special accounts salesmen may be called application or product specialists or consultants. In most cases the special accounts salesman will be more experienced and technically knowledgeable. He will tend to have higher level contact with the customer than his area salesman counterpart.

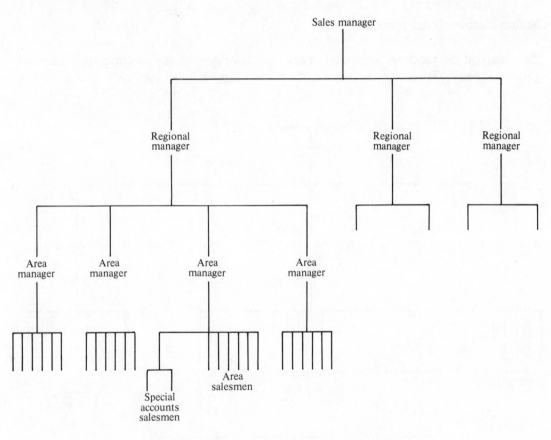

Figure 3.2   The special accounts salesman

The main advantage of this type of organisation structure is that it brings additional resources to bear on major customers with minimum disruption of traditional lines of reporting. However, for large customers operating in locations across a number of regions, the sales effort is still fragmented. Further, the status of the special accounts salesman may be insufficiently high for him to be able to influence the sales support function or have sufficient credibility in the eyes of senior customer management.

To help overcome some of these problems, the special accounts salesman is sometimes upgraded to become a regional accounts executive, reporting directly to the regional manager. Frequently these positions remain when the company moves towards the type of organisation structure discussed next, with the regional account executive being responsible for implementation of policy agreed by the national account executive and handling his own major regional customers.

The special accounts salesman type of organisation goes some way towards matching the criteria laid down in section 3.2. However, ultimately many suppliers have found it unsatisfactory for a number of reasons. In particular, since the task of selling to major customers is very different from that of selling to smaller customers in terms of its complexity and time scale, so the task of sales management varies likewise. Thus, first and second line sales management must manage both activities differently, a task which often proves to be difficult, except for the very able manager, and in many cases the special accounts salesmen fail to receive the supervision they require. This causes further problems of communication, overlap of activity, job specification and co-ordination.

National accounts department

This method of tackling large customers has its origins in the fast moving consumer goods industry. Typically the organisation structure will be as shown in Figure 3.3.

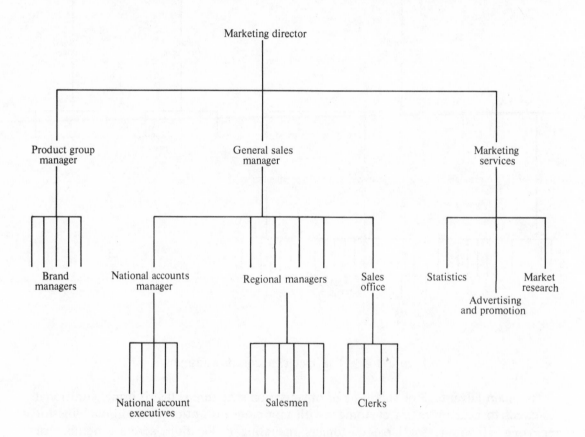

Figure 3.3   The national accounts department

The major customers will be the direct responsibility of the national accounts department which is headed by a national accounts manager who reports directly to the general sales manager. Reporting to the national accounts manager will be a number of national account executives each of whom will have a number of customers, usually between three and ten. The job of the national account executive is to call on the head office of the customer and initiate and co-ordinate all special activity directed at him. However, for the practical implementation of this activity he relies to a large extent on the regional managers and field salesmen and to a lesser extent on marketing services and brand management. For example, the national account executive may negotiate a special promotion with the head office buyer of a major multiple. This means that the retailer's divisional managers and store managers will be notified accordingly by head office. However, it is for the regional managers and field salesmen to follow this up and sell the promotion into each division and store. The assistance of marketing services may be required to provide special stands, stickers and display material and to produce data on the effectiveness of the promotion.

This type of organisation structure generally evolves through a number of stages. Initially it will be a response to the need for co-ordinating activity towards major customers.

Typically one or a few national account executives will be positioned slightly above the existing salesmen in the organisation structure, but below the first line managers. This structure will be a step forward, but it still has a number of disadvantages. Relating it to the criteria for an effective organisation structure, established in section 3.2, it is clearly more market oriented, better related to the task to be carried out, increases commitment to particular customers and facilitates company policy. However, since more personnel are involved and new roles need to be established, there may be additional problems with overlap of activity, clarity of job specifications and ease of communications. Sometimes these problems are compounded by the way the new organisation is introduced and this is why some companies regress to a purely geographic-oriented sales organisation.

If the supplier is reasonably satisfied with the results obtained from this initial type of structure, he will usually seek to strengthen it so that it begins to move towards that shown in Figure 3.2. The major account activity is put under a manager and the whole activity upgraded in organisational status. The national account executives will be on a level with the first line sales managers. This will increase their ability to influence the field sales activity, and facilitate communication and co-ordination with product management and marketing services.

As a result the effectiveness with which major customers' tasks are co-ordinated and carried out is increased. As the major accounts department grows in strength and status, the company systems will be increasingly oriented to its needs, thus reducing the overlap of activities, clarifying job specifications, easing communication and ensuring that all necessary information is channelled through the national accounts executive. This makes the job of the national accounts executive more complex since he becomes much more than a super salesman. He must continue to sell, but he must also co-ordinate, manage, influence, analyse and plan much more carefully than before. The criteria on which his performance is judged will likewise become more complex.

The third stage of development of this type of structure is to further strengthen the national accounts department by including field salesmen and some marketing services staff in it. The department will be headed by a general manager – major accounts, reporting to the marketing director at the same level or even above the general sales manager. This organisation structure is the logical response to a company policy of maintaining a large proportion of its sales with relatively few major customers. It further concentrates company resources around the important customers and thus makes the activity easier to co-ordinate and control. It further recognises explicitly that major customers require to be marketed to individually. This means that marketing services and, to a large extent, product management, must gear their activity accordingly, decreasing their use of broad-brush marketing tools, such as national advertising, and increasing their use of specific weapons such as in-store promotions. The field sales resources within the national accounts department are likewise geared to implement the customer sales and marketing plans in the most important outlets of each major customer. Clearly, these changes reduce the nature, scale and operating methods of the traditional field sales operation under the general sales manager which must be carefully considered before the new structure is implemented.

Market oriented organisation

Most organisations sell to a number of different market segments. Many have developed a structure to mirror the differences between their various markets and have a separate department handling each. In some cases the market segment may be made up of a few large customers. A typical example is a computer manufacturer which has a division dealing solely with Government. If the sales and profit potential is large enough then the department could have its own production, credit control, and development, as well as marketing sections. This type of structure takes the general manager – national accounts structure one step further than described earlier. However, it is only applicable where it is possible to split completely the various segments, with no overlap since each department will tend to operate autonomously. The ultimate example is where there is only one supplier and one customer. This is the case for a UK manufacturer of a particular type of vehicle suspension system which is used by only one motor manufacturer.

The evolution of organisation structure

The three different types of organisation structure illustrated above each represent the supplier's response to the increasing importance of major customers. Initially the response will be a low level one, the special accounts salesman. As the customer increases in importance so the rationale for the national accounts department becomes more compelling. Finally the market-oriented structure is most appropriate in response to the customer's overpowering importance.

It is vital to realise, however, that the cause and effect relationship works both ways. The increasing importance of major customers influences organisation structure which will improve the service to these customers and hence the amount of profitable business obtained; this results in a further increase in their importance.

The supplier, therefore, can create an organisational mechanism which will force him to spiral towards the situation where fewer and fewer customers account for more and more of his business. The best way of avoiding this eventuality is to develop an explicit customer mix policy as shown in Chapter 2. Unless this policy is taken into account in deciding the most appropriate structure, a dangerous pitfall lies in wait for the company.

3.5 SUMMARY

This chapter has shown that it is not possible to generalise about the type of structure a supplier needs to tackle his major accounts or on how it should be organised and managed. In some situations it may be possible to form complete departments around specific customer groups. In many cases, however, this is unlikely to be practical. Where it is not possible to bring the various tasks together in one department, then the problems of management co-ordination and control are more difficult. This is because the activities of a number of different functional specialists have to be co-ordinated.

Where no separate department exists that incorporates all the necessary functions, then there may be considerable difficulty in co-ordinating the necessary activity. Considerable tact, persuasion and patience is often required to bring about the desired result. To assess the effectiveness of the current and any proposed future structures for dealing with major customers, the manager should refer to the following seven criteria:

(a) company policy;
(b) the market;
(c) the task to be carried out;
(d) minimum overlap of activity;
(e) clear job specification;
(f) ease of communications;
(g) the concept of commitment.

Where the existing organisation structure does not match these criteria adequately then a new structure must be evolved by identifying:

(a) the task to be carried out;
(b) the number of staff required;
(c) how their efforts should be co-ordinated;
(d) who is responsible for major customers.

In many instances, after carrying out such an analysis, companies have (for the first time):

(a) established how many people are involved in servicing major customers;
(b) highlighted the vital importance of co-ordinating their efforts;
(c) substantially increased the awareness of all personnel of the importance of their role vis-à-vis major customers.

Finally, the different sorts of organisational responses have been discussed and how such structures evolve. This has re-emphasised the need for companies to develop an explicit customer mix policy.

Action planning checklist

Questions	Answers and action	Timing of action and evaluation
1 How well does the current organisation structure which handles major customers rate against the criteria?		
2 What services must be provided for major customers?		
3 Which employees deal with major customers?		
4 What changes are required in present staffing levels and job specifications?		
5 How are the efforts of individuals to be co-ordinated to achieve optimal results with major customers?		

4
Analysing customer profitability

4.1 INTRODUCTION

The effectiveness of the effort directed by the company towards major accounts cannot be judged solely in terms of the sales volume generated. The company is in business mainly to generate profit and its profit and loss account illustrates the profitability of the total business. However, because it represents an aggregation of the component parts of the company, it does not show how profitable each of the parts are, and it does not highlight the areas for potential action.

Major customers who represent a large part of the company's business will be responsible for generating or failing to generate a significant part of its profit. If a supplier is to increase the profit he earns from his large customers, and effectively control the effort directed at them, then it is vital that he understands the nature of the profit mechanism that operates. That is not to say that major customer profitability provides the sole criterion for decision making, but it is a very important factor and one which experience indicates management rarely calculate and hence usually omit from their considerations.

For example, when a consumer goods supplier is considering a price promotion with a multiple retailer it is rare for the total impact on customer profitability to be evaluated. The effectiveness of the promotion is usually judged on the additional gross margins generated by the additional sales obtained. Rarely, however, are the additional costs of distribution, selling, credit and administration taken into account. Even more rarely will the effect of the additional sales during the promotion period be judged against the loss of business in subsequent periods to establish the net effect on profit. Most companies will have a product costing system which will tell them how much profit individual products are contributing. On the basis of this information decisions will be made on product rationalisation and on how to allocate investment and manpower resources. The concept of major customer costing adds a further and vitally important dimension to the product costing concept in determining the way the company allocates its resources.

This chapter explains how to evaluate major customer profitability and how to use the resultant information. It is intended to assist the senior manager in developing the system and help the sales manager understand its uses and limitations.

4.2 CONCEPT OF CUSTOMER PROFITABILITY

Management will also be familiar with the contribution, trading and profit and loss account which identifies the revenues and costs across the whole business or the particular operating unit. Likewise the product profit and loss account identifies the revenues and costs associated with a particular product.

Most senior managers will get an operating statement on a monthly basis which will show the revenues and costs their departments or divisions have incurred. Under a budgetary control system comparison will be made against budget for each item.

In interpreting the figures, management will take into account how the costs are made up. In particular, differentiation will be made between fixed and variable costs, direct and indirect costs. Variable costs are those which vary in line with changing sales volume. Typical examples are raw materials and packaging. Fixed costs are those which do not vary over a period of time (usually one year) with changing sales volumes. Typical examples are management salaries and rent. Semi-fixed (or semi-variable) costs are those which vary with changing volume sales, but not *pro rata*. Typical examples are distribution costs and financing costs. Direct costs are those which are directly attributable to a specific entity such as a product, department or customer. These costs can be fixed or variable. For example, the marketing director's salary is directly attributable to the marketing department. Indirect costs are those which cannot be attributed to a specific entity.

It should be noted that a cost can be direct relative to one entity and indirect relative to another. For example, the cost of warehousing can be a direct distribution cost but an indirect product and customer cost. The divisional managing director's costs are an indirect department cost (overhead) but a direct divisional cost.

Similar principles apply to the customer profit and loss account. In looking at major customer profitability it is necessary to identify the relevant costs and revenue associated with servicing these customers and then allocate them in an appropriate way. The method of allocation and its accuracy will vary considerably from company to company and amongst the various cost headings. Thus, for example, advertising costs may be allocated by one company to a customer on the basis of sales to them, as a proportion of total sales. This is undoubtedly a reasonable way of allocating such costs, but whether it is accurate is questionable. To establish accuracy it is necessary to look into the precise function that advertising performs in the particular company. For example, (a) does it focus on specific products or is it corporate; (b) does trade and channel advertising take place; (c) does advertising support or replace personal sales effort? It is then possible to establish how the costs can be allocated more accurately. In reality, whether the costs are in fact allocated on this basis depends on the cost and time associated with making the allocation. If considerable amounts of additional records have to be kept and new systems developed then the extra costs may exceed the benefits from the extra accuracy obtained.

The following sections discuss the basis for making cost allocations and the reader will be able to relate his own situation to them and judge the likely levels of inaccuracy that will occur. However, in spite of the ambiguities of some cost allocations and subsequent loss of accuracy, it is wise for suppliers to attempt such allocations in order to get some measure of effectiveness and efficiency. Undoubtedly it is better to have some information, however limited, than none at all. The fact that it is not perfect information should not invalidate the exercise. Conversely, the fact that precise numbers appear on the paper should not lull the manager into believing they are accurate. In short, for profitability analyses to be of real value, management must be aware of both their benefits and their limitations.

4.3 METHODOLOGY OF MAJOR ACCOUNT PROFITABILITY ANALYSIS

Before considering the practical problems of carrying out the profitability analysis it is useful to look at the principles involved using a simplified example. An industrial company is concerned to establish the revenues and costs attached to its top three customers who account for 60 per cent of its sales. To maintain simplicity, it is assumed the company only sells one product. The analysis should be tackled in six steps:

1 Identify customer turnover and volume sales.
2 Establish all directly variable costs.
3 Identify all functional expenses.
4 Assign functional expenses to customers.
5 Prepare customer profit and loss account.
6 Analyse the profit and loss account.

Step 1: identify customer turnover and volume sales

It is first necessary to establish the level of sales to each customer together with the number of units sold, as shown in Table 4.1.

Table 4.1   Quarterly sales volume and value

Customer:	A	B	C	All customers
Sales	£300,000	£100,000	£200,000	£1,000,000
Unit volume	20,000	6,667	13,333	66,667

These sales were obtained over a period of time, a quarter, and the figures refer to the previous quarter. Generally, customer profitability analyses are carried out on a quarterly basis with an annual summary. If required the calculations could be done more frequently, e.g. on a monthly basis.

Step 2: establish all directly variable costs

These are the costs which are directly attributable to the customer and vary in line with changes in sales volume to the customer. This includes discounts and, of course, cost of goods sold. (It may include other costs which are discussed in the next section.) The schedule of these costs is shown in Table 4.2.

Table 4.2   Schedule of directly variable costs

Customer:	A	B	C	All customers
Discounts	£90,000	£28,000	£80,000	£250,000
C.O.G.S.	£156,000	£52,000	£104,000	£520,000

Step 3: identify all functional expenses

Usually expenses are accounted for under such headings as salaries, purchases, interest, depreciation, rent. If these expenses are to be allocated to the customer, it is necessary first to identify the functional areas and allocate the expenses against these functions.

Assuming there are three expense headings (salaries, rent and purchases, e.g. promotional material, stationery) and four functional expense headings (sales force, advertising, distribution and invoicing), the task is to allocate each expense to one functional heading.

Take salaries as an example. There are five salesmen, one advertising manager and secretary, two delivery drivers and a warehouseman and five invoicing clerks and a credit manager. Table 4.3 shows how salaries are allocated, based on the number and type of employee to each functional area. Rent and purchases may be allocated in a similar way.

Table 4.3   Expense allocation to function

£	Total	Sales force	Advertising	Distribution	Invoicing
Salaries	93,000	51,000	12,000	14,000	16,000
Rent	30,000	–	4,000	20,000	6,000
Purchases	35,000	4,000	15,000	14,000	2,000
	£158,000	£55,000	£31,000	£48,000	£24,000

Since all the salesmen work away from the office and no space is set aside for them there, the sales force is not allocated any rent expenses. Most of the rent goes to distribution since the warehouse and despatch take up the largest amount of floor space. A smaller general office houses the invoicing section, and the advertising manager and his secretary have an office and a small store room. Finally the purchases account is split between the four functional headings. This account includes such items as media and print costs, stationery, fuel, lighting and heating, and trade exhibitions.

As a result of the analysis, the £158,000 of expenses has been reclassified against the various relevant functional expenses.

Step 4: assign functional expenses to customers

The task is now to determine how much of the functional activity has gone into servicing each customer. Thus, when considering the sales force it is necessary to determine how much of the total cost of £55,000 it is reasonable to attribute to customers A, B and C. On what basis should such an allocation take place? A number of possibilities exist:

1 As a proportion of turnover accounted for by each customer.
2 As a proportion of the number of sales calls received by each account related to the number of calls on all customers.
3 As a proportion of the total sales time taken up by each customer including travelling time.
4 As a proportion of the total face to face sales time taken by each customer.

It is assumed that in the example cited senior management decides that an allocation based on the number of visits, for which they already have records, will be more realistic than on the basis of turnover. Since there are no records detailing how the sales force spends its time, any allocation on a time basis is currently not possible, although it would be most accurate and would involve the sales force in additional paperwork if it were implemented in the future. Thus, sales force costs will be allocated on number of sales calls made. Table 4.4 shows how all the functional expenses are allocated.

Table 4.4   Allocation to customers of functional expenses

Customer	Sales force No. of sales calls per quarter	Advertising Sales turnover per quarter	Distribution Sales volume per quarter	Invoicing Number of orders per quarter
A	40	300,000	20,000	30
B	35	100,000	6,667	28
C	10	200,000	13,333	2
Total Co.	975	£1,000,000	66,667	4,000
Functional expense	£55,000	£31,000	£48,000	£24,000
No. of units	975	£1,000,000	66,667	4,000
=	£56.4	£0.031	£0.72	£6

Since advertising was spread across all customers it was allocated on the basis of sales value of each customer. Since the products are fairly bulky, distribution costs are allocated on the basis of sales volume. Invoicing costs are directly related to the number of orders.

Step 5: prepare customer profit and loss account

It is now possible to prepare major customer profit and loss accounts as shown in Table 4.5. First the directly variable costs are deducted from sales leaving a customer gross profit. The expenses are then allocated by multiplying the functional expense per unit (evaluated in step 4) by the number of units appropriate to that customer. When the total expenses are deducted from the customer gross contribution, the result obtained is the net trading profit.

Table 4.5   Customer profit and loss accounts

	A	B	C	Company total
Sales	300,000	100,000	200,000	1,000,000
Discounts	90,000	28,000	80,000	250,000
Cost of goods sold	156,000	52,000	104,000	520,000
Customer gross profit	54,000	20,000	16,000	230,000
Expenses:				
Sales force (£56.4 per call)	2,256	1,974	564	55,000
Advertising (£0.031 per £ sales)	9,300	3,100	6,200	31,000
Distribution (£0.72 per unit sold)	14,400	4,800	9,600	48,000
Invoicing (£6 per order)	180	168	12	24,000
Total expenses	26,136	10,042	16,376	158,000
Net trading profit (loss)	27,864	9,958	(376)	72,000

Step 6: analyse the profit and loss account

A review of the three profit and loss accounts for customers A, B and C shows an interesting picture. Customer A, who accounts for 30 per cent of company turnover, is responsible for only 23 per cent of the company's gross profit, but nearly 40 per cent of its net trading profit. Customer C, on the other hand, who accounts for 20 per cent of total company sales and 7 per cent of customer gross profit, represents a slight net trading loss. A review of customer B's performance shows that whilst it accounts for only 10 per cent of turnover and less than 9 per cent of customer gross profit, it is responsible for 14 per cent of net trading profit.

Thus, around 55 per cent of the company's net trading profit is made up by two customers who account for 40 per cent of turnover. The value of developing the customer profit and loss account should now be apparent. Although the whole company is trading profitably, making £72,000 in the quarter, this overall figure hides a number of problems. What action should management take? Several alternatives are possible, as explained below.

Drop customer C
This dramatic decision might be made on the basis that it would eliminate a loss making customer and hence increase overall profitability. The decision maker would, however, be putting a lot more faith in the meaning of the figures than they deserve. Would advertising expenses, for instance, be reduced in proportion to the loss in associated sales revenue? It might be argued that some reduction in advertising might take place but would it amount to £6,200, particularly since this figure contains a proportion of the £16,000 of salaries and rent of the advertising department? Therefore, it seems likely that although advertising expenditure might be reduced if customer C were dropped, the net effect would be to increase the advertising expense allocations to customers A and B.

Increase profitability of customer C
Examination of the profit and loss accounts shows that the main reason for C's negative net trading position is the high level of discount it enjoys. This has been obtained on the basis of placing extremely large, but few, orders. Only two orders were placed in the quarter under consideration, accounting for £200,000 of sales, i.e. average order value £100,000. This compares with average order values of £10,000 and £3,750 for customers A and B respectively. Clearly with the prospect of such a large carrot the sales department have given a very large discount to get the order. Unfortunately, because of the nature of the product (high volume to weight ratio) and the numerous locations at which customer C expects delivery, the costs of distribution are no lower than for customers A and B.

It seems clear that the key to improving customer C's profitability is to negotiate improved terms with him. This is by no means an easy task for the salesman involved, particularly since C represents 20 per cent of the company's sales revenue and doubtless considerably more of the revenue of the sales territory concerned. However, by using the information and resources he has available in a planned and co-ordinated fashion, the salesman should be able to carry out this difficult task. Subsequent chapters discuss in detail how he can set about it.

Reduce dependence on customer A
Although management has every reason to be pleased with the profit that customer A

produces for the company, it does substantially increase its dependence on this customer. With 30 per cent of sales and nearly 40 per cent of net trading profit, customer A is indeed very important. Should it choose to use its power there is relatively little the company can do at this point in time. If it demands an extra 5 per cent discount (hearing that customer C is getting substantially more than it enjoys) the effect will be to more than halve its net trading profit and knock over 20 per cent off the overall company trading profit. This might be sufficient to put the whole company in the red for the quarter.

Alternatively, customer A might offer an inducement. For example, the buyer may indicate that another £100,000 of orders would be forthcoming but that an extra 5 per cent discount on all business would be required. This might appear very tempting to the salesman, although much less so once the effect on net trading profit is evaluated. However, the implications of the overall company risk profile are considerable and significantly worsen the situation. Again the need for a company to have an explicit statement of its policy (Chapter 2) is apparent.

Therefore, reducing dependence on customer A, appears to be vital and this could be brought about in a number of ways including those now listed.

1. Increase sales to customer B.
2. Increase sales to smaller customers who currently take between £50,000 and £100,000 of sales. Careful identification of these customers will be required and then planning the approach and committing company resources to achieve the plan. Targetting of the sales force relative to these accounts, allocating priority distribution, ear-marking stock and so on may be necessary.
3. Open up other market segments, i.e. export.
4. Develop new applications.
5. Develop new products.

Increase dependence of customer A

It may be felt that customer A would not be tempted to use its power if it relied more on its supplier. If the company were offering a unique or semi-unique product with no direct competitors this might work. However, if a number of direct competitors exist this will be a difficult policy to follow, although it does not mean that the supplier should avoid entrenching itself with customer A in terms of the technical support it gives and its level of service, for example. However, the short term cost of these must be calculated and set against customer A to evaluate the effect on trading profit.

Increase sales to customer B

This approach is worthwhile for two reasons. Customer B's trading profit ratio (10 per cent on sales) is very good and increased sales should have a very beneficial effect on profit and will help reduce the company's dependence on company A. How this can be brought about will be discussed in subsequent chapters.

4.4 USING THE PROFITABILITY ANALYSIS

Having determined the profitability of the major customers the information should be used in a number of ways.

Assessment of comparative profitability

The analysis is likely to show varying levels of profitability between different customers who have similar magnitudes of gross sales value. The reasons for this can be identified by detailed examination of the profit and loss accounts. It may be due to varying levels of discounts or to different calling frequencies of sales staff, or variations between the length of credit taken, for example.

The analysis thus provides a yardstick against which actual profitability of individual accounts can be measured and the means of identifying the main reasons for any shortfall.

Assessment of comparative performance

Comparison between the revenue/cost structure of the various major customers will give a guide as to the effectiveness of the resources used to service any particular customer. For example, customer A may produce £20,000 revenue for every £100 of direct selling cost. Customer B may only produce £10,000 for the same direct selling cost. The average for all major customers may be £15,000. The manager can now see that the salesman looking after customer A appears to be twice as effective as the one looking after B, and significantly better than the average. Further analysis will show why.

Similarly, other cost elements such as distribution, advertising, incentives and debtors can be compared and action taken to improve the effectiveness of this expenditure with individual major customers.

A basis for planning and control

The planning process needed to market effectively to major customers is described in Chapter 5. The profitability analysis provides a key input into this process by establishing the current profit position. The analysis will help in determining the future profit objectives and the impact of changing product mix, marketing and sales activity, price and sales volume on these objectives.

Allocation of resources

With limited resources of time, people and money at his disposal, the manager is faced with the challenge of allocating them as effectively as possible between a multitude of competing opportunities. An important consideration in determining where these resources should be applied is the profit generated. By means of the customer profitability analysis, the sales manager can decide how he should deploy his sales force and spend the discretionary parts of his sales budget by allocating priority to those customers where the largest increases in profit can be achieved.

Allocation of resources must take place within the overall policy guidelines laid down by senior management. A marginally profitable customer should not be abandoned if, by so doing, the overall company risk exposure is increased to an unacceptable level. However, as discussed in Chapter 2, customer profitability is one input in determining company policy. Profitability analysis will not only help the sales manager but also the marketing director in deciding how to allocate the company's resources.

4.5   INTRODUCTION OF ACCOUNT PROFITABILITY ANALYSIS

The example given will have shown the reader the substantial benefit to be derived from evaluating account profitability on a regular basis. Frequently it enables disparate reporting formats, containing a variety of information, to be replaced by one form.

Nevertheless, there is often considerable resistance within the company to the introduction of such a system. It is as well to be aware of the objections which have been raised in real life so that these can be taken account of during implementation.

Some common objections

'It's just another lot of figures.'

Executives, and particularly sales executives often feel they are inundated with computer printouts, returns, analyses and so on. To them, the customer profit and loss accounts just represent another lot of figures. Therefore, it is important to review existing information received and decide which parts can be replaced by the new system.

'What if it shows all my major accounts are unprofitable?'

This is often the fear felt by salesmen and sales managers, although it is not necessarily stated out loud. It is important to reassure all staff as to the purpose and use of the figures. Just because a major account is unprofitable it will not be dropped, nor will it imply that the salesman responsible has performed badly. It signifies that the salesman and sales management will have their performance judged on how they manage to increase profit or reduce loss with particular accounts within the overall policy constraints laid down by senior management. Clearly this has implications for the objective setting and planning process which will be discussed in subsequent chapters.

'I don't understand what use the figures will be.'

This is another part of the first objection ('just another lot of figures'), but it indicates clearly the need to ensure that all staff who have to work with the system are trained in its use. In particular they must understand:

(a) the purpose in providing the information;
(b) how to analyse the data;
(c) the limitations of the figures;
(d) how to draw up action plans as a result of the analyses.

'It will involve a lot of extra paperwork.'

In most cases the relevant base data will be available to enable the necessary cost allocations to be made with acceptable accuracy. In situations where this is not so then it is likely that additional systems will have to be set up anyway if management is to be able to effectively control the business, irrespective of whether account profitability information is supplied or not. Thus, the effect of introducing a major account profitability analysis is to focus attention on the fact that such basic information is really needed.

There will be a need for the base data to be accumulated and analysed in slightly different ways which will probably be the responsibility of the finance department or marketing services department. In time, once the system is in operation it may be decided to increase the accuracy with which the costs are allocated. This will involve some additional paperwork. For example, if it is more realistic to allocate sales force costs on the basis of time spent with each customer then it will be necessary for the salesmen to record this information, when previously they might just record that a visit was made. Generally, the amount of additional paperwork is small and will only be undertaken if the associated benefit outweighs the additional costs involved.

It is important that any additional paperwork be carefully introduced to the relevant staff and training given in how to correctly complete the documentation.

'Management will soon want me to report back when I sneeze.'
There is sometimes a feeling, particularly on the part of sales personnel, that all this reporting, analysis, computer print-outs and so on is getting in the way of the basic selling job and that, provided the sales are obtained, management ought not to be concerned with how the sales force spends it time or who it calls on. Although this description is a slight caricature of the real life situation, it does encourage management to consider and communicate the benefits of the reporting procedures to those who have to do the reporting.

4.6 PRACTICAL EXAMPLES OF MAJOR ACCOUNT PROFITABILITY ANALYSIS

In developing a profit and loss account for each of its major customers, every company must develop its own format. To do so requires a detailed examination of all cost and revenue areas and the assistance of the financial department.

Consumer goods company

An example typical of the fast moving consumer goods industry is shown in Table 4.6. Each element will be examined in detail to assist the reader to develop the format most suitable to his own organisation. As far as possible this format should fit in with the normal manner in which the company lays out its accounts.

Table 4.6   Example of contribution and trading profit account for consumer goods company

CUSTOMER		
	£ TOTAL	% GSV
1 Gross sales value		
2 Less: Invoiced discounts		
3 Net sales		
4 Less: Manufacturing cost		
5 : Distribution		
6 Customer gross profit		
7 Less: Sales allowances		
8 : Marketing allowances		
9 : Consumer deals		
10 : Other marketing*		
11 Customer contribution		
12 Less: Direct sales force		
13 : Sales overheads*		
14 : Marketing overheads*		
15 : General and administration*		
16 Trading profit		
17 Less: Payment discount		
18 : Debtor interest		
19 : Stock interest		
20 Profit after interest		

*Allocations

Starting with the sales revenue at the top of the account, costs are allocated in descending order of directness. First the costs specifically identified with sales to the particular customer are deducted, such as discounts and manufacturing cost, i.e. directly variable costs. Next direct costs associated with servicing the customer are deducted. These costs are currently likely to be accumulated under various functional expense headings, such as sales allowances and marketing expenditure. Overheads are allocated next and, finally, the interest charge associated with financing the business with the customer is deducted. At each stage different levels of profit are obtained, ranging from customer gross profit at the highest level to profit after interest at the bottom of the account.

Line 1: gross sales value
This refers to the value of sales if they were charged at the maximum possible price. Some possible definitions are:

(a) invoiced sales at full list price/trade price;
(b) invoiced sales at full list price less returns and ullages;
(c) order input at full list price;
(d) invoiced sales plus additional revenues obtained from service, marketing contribution, training reimbursement, etc.

Line 2: invoiced discounts
These are generally the normal or standard discounts to the customer. Some possible definitions are:

(a) all discounts and allowances related to customer;
(b) all discounts, allowances and credits.

This cost item should include all monies which are taken off the full gross/list/trade price and all monies returned to the customer by way of overriders and bonuses, for example. In some cases discounts may be built into the invoiced price which appears at the top of the invoice to the customer, i.e. the computer has been programmed to calculate the list price less the basic or standard customer discount for invoicing purposes and only that discounted figure is printed. Great care should be taken to add back the discount to obtain gross sales value and to include it in invoiced discounts.

Line 3: net sales
This figure is obtained after the deduction of invoiced discounts and represents the revenue the supplier receives from the customer concerned out of which it must pay all other costs and make a profit.

Line 4: manufacturing costs/cost of goods sold
These are the product manufacturing costs as determined by the cost accountants. This is normally taken as ex-factory or landed cost. To evaluate this cost, the volume of sales of each product to the customer must be identified and multiplied by the associated product cost.

Where revenue is obtained from other sources such as service, repair, spare parts, the cost of providing these should also be included.

Line 5: distribution/transportation/delivery
The correct position of distribution costs in the account is a matter requiring careful

consideration. The normal layout of the company's trading account may be inappropriate for a variety of reasons.

The direct costs of distribution are regarded in this example as being associated with the manufacture of the product and getting it to the customer, and hence separate from the marketing effort. Often, particularly with industrial companies, a separate charge is levied for delivery. When using a contract haulier the charge can be included in the invoiced price, and hence in line 1 of the account. Therefore, it may be put higher up in the account and then deducted from gross sales revenue to obtain net sales. Other companies may wish to treat distribution costs as part of the marketing activity and hence subject to variation depending on management decision. If this were so it would appear further down the profit and loss account.

The direct distribution costs are those incurred specifically in servicing the particular customer and will include delivery costs but not warehousing or distribution management. Where a supplier operates a van sales operation then it is usually not possible to split sales and distribution costs.

Relevant types of costs include (a) driver's wages and national insurance, (b) fuel and oil, (c) repair and maintenance, (d) tyres and spare parts, (e) supervisor's wages and national insurance (proportion of time spent on relief delivery for example), (f) depreciation.

Where contract hauliers are used the delivery costs are relatively easy to ascertain. Where a company has its own vehicles, there are a number of ways in which direct distribution costs can be allocated including (a) per mile, (b) per tonne, (c) per case, (d) per delivery, (e) per hour. Whenever possible true allocation units should be used, i.e. actual number of hours, miles or cases. Thus, if a customer has two warehouses, for example in Reading and Glasgow, it is necessary to measure the actual return mileage or hours from the supplier's depot. This is relatively simple on single drop deliveries but becomes more complex on multidrop delivery runs. In such cases it is often useful to draw zones of increasing distance around the depots, reflecting as much as possible delivery routes, allocating standard costs per zone on a mileage, travelling time or other realistic basis. The distribution costs for, say, customer X can be evaluated as follows:

(a) number of customer X delivery points in zone 1;
(b) cost per drop in zone 1;
(c) cost per period ((a) × (b) × number of drops per period).

Costs for other zones can be evaluated similarly.

It may be necessary to differentiate yet again between different types of delivery, even in the same zone. For example, it may take twice as long to deliver to one type of customer compared to another even though they are in the same area and take similar quantities of product. This could arise for a number of reasons including difficulty of access, queueing, incidence of refused deliveries. The standard methods of allocation discussed above would not differentiate between them. However, to reflect the real situation it will be necessary to weight particular categories of customer to ensure they receive a fair allocation of the delivery costs that they incur. The main variable cost element will be driver costs and depreciation since all other costs will be unaffected by the vehicle waiting longer. To take this factor into account, the additional driver and depreciation costs associated with the extra waiting time for each category of account must be subtracted from the total costs before allocating all direct delivery expenses, and then they must again be added against each category.

In many cases it is easy to become overwhelmed by the complexity of allocating delivery costs. The more precise are the attempts, the greater the amounts of data produced, the higher the cost and the longer the time taken for analysis to occur. Thus, there is considerable merit in keeping the basis of allocation as simple as possible, making allowances for lack of accuracy in the interpretation of the figures.

Line 6: customer gross profit

This figure is obtained by deducting manufacturing and distribution costs from net sales. It represents the amount the customer contributes to the company's fixed and semi-variable costs, and the amount available to cover the main discretionary items of marketing expenditure.

Line 7: sales allowances

Most large customers will benefit from discounts, rebates, allowances and commissions over and above the standard terms enjoyed which are negotiated by the salesman with the buyer. Certain types of allowances and discounts will be shown on the invoice and included in line 2. Others such as promotional bonuses, merchandising bonus, and collection allowances may not be shown. In the example given this category of sales allowance refers to money back arrangements that are not shown on the invoice.

The process of identifying all discounts and allowances is often a very long and difficult one. In some cases particular customers will receive certain benefits which were established many years ago. The reason for this benefit has long ceased to be apparent and as a result the discount proves difficult to find. However, it is vital that every effort is made to uncover all such allowances. This will entail extensive investigation and discussion with sales staff, sales office staff, accountants and general management.

Line 8: marketing allowances

These are not dissimilar to sales allowances in the sense that they reflect the marketing activity directly attributable to the particular customer. This may include items such as (a) joint advertising, (b) special exhibitions, (c) demonstrations, (d) in-store representation, (e) seminars, (f) films, (g) new product development. In many industrial situations special material is produced to support the selling effort to develop applications in particular industries. Thus, if a film, product brochures, seminars and training were developed for the UK steel industry then such marketing effort could rightly be allocated to the British Steel Corporation.

Line 9: consumer deals

In fast moving consumer goods companies this generally refers to 'money off' offers and 'flash packs'. Industrial companies often have similar offers to their customers to clear excessive stocks or to boost sales at the end of a sales period.

Line 10: other marketing

These costs are allocated generally on the basis of gross sales value as a proportion of total sales. However, additional refinements may be necessary to take account of varying product mixes. They include advertising, general promotional activity, sales support material, general exhibitions and so on, i.e. broad scale marketing designed to generate sales which cannot be directly allocated to any particular customer.

The rationale for including these costs at this point in the account is that items of expenditure such as advertising are designed to increase sales with the end user. The more product the customer purchases, which he in turn sells, the greater will be the advantage he gains from the advertising and hence the higher the cost he should bear.

For a supplier selling direct to the end user such as an industrial or service company, there is less logic in allocating such marketing costs in this manner and they are often included in marketing overheads further down the profit and loss account.

Line 11: customer contribution
By deducting all allowances, deals and other marketing expenditure from customer gross profit, customer contribution is obtained. This represents the amount available to cover the fixed and semi-fixed costs associated with the customer.

Line 12: direct sales force costs
Table 4.7 shows a convenient format for evaluating sales force costs. The use of this form can best be illustrated by an example.

Table 4.7   Sales force costs

CUSTOMER . . . . TURNOVER £ . . . .
Management contact costs
1   Head office management   £ . . . .
2   Field management   £ . . . .
3   Cost per period   £
Sales force calls
4   No. of type A contact   . . . .
5   Calls per year   . . . .
6   Cost per call   £ . . . .
7   Cost per period   £
8   No. of type B contact   . . . .
9   Calls per year   . . . .
10   Cost per call   £ . . . .
11   Cost per period   £
12   No. of type C contact   . . . .
13   Calls per year   . . . .
14   Cost per call   £ . . . .
15   Cost per period   £
Other calls (e.g. merchandising, demonstrations, pioneering, technical services, customer engineering, etc.)
16   No. of contacts   . . . .
17   Calls per year   . . . .
18   Cost per call   £ . . . .
19   Cost per period   £
20   Total sales force costs   £
(3 + 7 + 11 + 15 + 19)

First it is necessary to establish the direct sales cost per hour. This is done as follows:

$$\text{Direct salesman cost} = \text{salary} + \text{bonus/incentive}$$
$$+ \text{ car} + \text{national insurance}$$
$$= \text{£10,000 p.a., say.}$$

Field sales management costs = £12,500 per manager.

Field sales management spend 20 per cent of their time selling and 80 per cent of their time supervising and training their salesmen.

Therefore, field sales management contact costs = £2,500 per manager.

Sales supervision cost = £10,000 per manager (i.e. 80 per cent of £12,500).

If each supervisor looks after eight salesmen, the supervisor
cost per salesman is $\dfrac{10,000}{8}$ = £1,250 p.a.

$$\text{Therefore total salesman cost} = \text{£10,000} + \text{£1,250}$$
$$= \text{£11,250 p.a.}$$
$$\text{per salesman.}$$

Assuming 220 working days = £51 per day or £7.30 per hour.

It is now necessary to establish the amount of time that head office management, field management and salesmen spend selling to the customer.

The head office contact should be readily ascertainable by establishing the time spent by the managing director, marketing director, sales director, major account executives, etc., on the particular major accounts, and allocating a proportion of their costs accordingly.

Having evaluated the field management costs, it is finally necessary to allocate them on the basis of the proportion of sales time spent with the particular customer.

The sales force cost can be more difficult to evaluate. If there is only one contact at one location then it is only necessary to establish the amount of time spent travelling to, and with, the contact to obtain a reasonable measure of sales force costs. However, most sales situations involve a variety of contacts at a number of different locations. For example, it may be necessary for an industrial sales force to call on the design engineer, project engineer, buyer, finance director and maintenance supervisor to obtain business. Each of these will require a different frequency of call which will be of different duration. The consumer products salesman will need to call at a number of different outlets of differing size belonging to the same multiple account. Each category of outlet will require a different call frequency and time spent per call depending on the sales potential. The format in Table 4.7 allows for three different categories of contact/outlet although additional categories may be necessary to suit industrial circumstances.

Finally it is necessary to evaluate other call costs, including service, installation and merchandising on a similar basis. Whether these costs are included in sales force costs or placed under a separate heading depends on their importance relative to the other sales costs. If they are sufficiently large, as in many industrial and consumer durable situations, being a profit centre in their own right, then it is sensible to represent them under a separate heading.

The total sales force cost is obtained by adding the management contact cost to the sales force cost per contact type, plus the other call costs.

To assess the realism of the various time estimates it is often advantageous to carry out an activity study of the sales force.

Lines 13, 14 and 15: sales overheads, marketing overheads, general and administration
These are the fixed costs such as rent, rates, insurance, salaries, pension, depreciation, research and electricity, associated with head office, sales, marketing, distribution, research and development, finance, credit control, etc., which are not directly attributable to particular customers. They are allocated generally on the basis of sales revenue or sales volume. Deduction of these costs and direct sales force costs from customer contribution leaves trading profit (line 16) which is available to cover financing costs.

Line 17: payment discount
If there is a discount allowed for prompt payment then this can be considered as a financing cost. Depending on the accounting convention within the organisation, however, it may be legitimate to consider it either as an invoiced discount (line 2) or a sales allowance (line 7).

Line 18: debtor interest
At the end of each month the customer is likely to have an amount it owes to the supplier, i.e. the amount outstanding on the monthly statement. This represents a financing cost for the supplier since he would be able to invest the cash either within his business or on deposit if it were available. Alternatively he may be able to reduce his bank overdraft by the amount outstanding.

The interest rate appropriate is a matter of judgement but could be one of the following: (a) overdraft rate, (b) standard internal rate on investment, (c) interest obtainable in the short term money market. The rate of interest needs to be reviewed at the end of each month to keep pace with any changes.

Line 19: stock interest
Generally it will be a supplier's policy to keep x weeks or months sales in stock to act as a buffer against unexpected surges in demand or interruptions in supply. Clearly, since capital is tied up, this policy has a cost associated with it. The interest rate considerations are the same as in debtor interest (line 18).

Line 20: profit after interest
Following the deduction of all financing costs the final profit figure after interest is arrived at. This represents the net profit after deducting all direct and fixed costs associated with that customer.

Industrial company

The contribution and trading profit account for a company selling products to manufacturing industry is shown in Table 4.8. Comparison with the account shown in Table 4.6 will show some similarities and interesting differences. In particular, since a contract haulier is used, delivery costs are included high up (line 4). Service revenue and costs are included as a separate entity in lines 16, 17 and 18, and financing costs (lines 20 and 21) are deducted before overhead allocations.

Table 4.8   Example of contribution and trading profit account for an
industrial product supplier

Customer. . . . .

Period . . . .

		£
1	Gross sales volume	
2	Less: Invoiced discounts	
3	: Credits	
4	: Delivery charges	
5	Net sales	_____
6	Less: Cost of goods sold	
7	: Product royalty	
8	Customer gross margin	_____
9	Less: Negotiated discount	
10	: Direct sales costs	
11	: Product trial costs	
12	: Installation costs	
13	: Invoicing costs	
14	: Customer operation training costs	
15	Customer gross contribution	_____
16	Add: Invoiced service and spares	
17	Less: Direct service costs	
18	: Spares costs	
19	Customer contribution	_____
20	Less: Debtor interest	
21	: Stock interest	
22	Operating profit	_____
23	Less: Sales overheads	
24	: Service overheads	
25	: Warehousing	
26	: General and administration	
27	Net profit	════════

Product profitability

In many cases it is desirable to identify the contribution made by each product or product group to the customer profitability. The format shown in Table 4.9 can be used to add this additional degree of sophistication. It is wise to restrict the analysis to not more than six product groups.

All costs directly applicable to the product are deducted before arriving at gross contribution figures, including an allocation of product advertising and promotion.

The benefit of producing the product profitability analysis is that it enables measurement to be made of the direct effect of (a) changes in product mix, (b) specific product promotional activity. This information can then be used by the salesman and sales manager to prepare sales plans and set objectives for the customer.

Table 4.9   Major customer product profit and loss analysis for period: . . .

Product group	A			B			C			Total		
	P.U.		%	P.U.		%	P.U.		%	P.U.		%
Sales volume Gross revenue Less: Off invoice discount : Credits Net sales			100			100			100			100
Less: Cost of sales Gross margin												
Less: Direct discount : Direct product promotion : Direct product audit												
Net margin												
Less: General product and advertising and promotion												
Gross contribution												

Note
P.U. = per unit

Cash and other discounts			
Trade incentive			
Direct sales costs			
Direct delivery costs			
Direct merchandising costs			
Other promotional and advertising costs			
Direct G and A cost			
M.B. factor			
Net contribution			
Interest and marketing overheads			

4.7 SUMMARY

This chapter has shown the methodology, format, uses and benefits of analysing major customer profitability. This should be tackled in six steps.

1   Identify customer turnover and volume sales.
2   Establish all directly variable costs.
3   Identify all functional expenses.

4   Assign functional expenses to customers.
5   Prepare the profit and loss account.
6   Analyse the account.

The previous sections have shown a variety of possible layouts for the major customer profit and loss statement. This demonstrates that each company must determine its own format according to the nature of its business and accounting conventions. This is a skilled exercise requiring experienced personnel.

In comparing the performance of a number of customers, management must be continually aware of the limitations of the figures and the special circumstances which might be relevant to one customer and not another. These special circumstances, which are not taken into account by the various mechanisms for accumulating and allocating costs, might lead management to increase or decrease particular cost figures. It is vital that management understands how the figures are compiled if they are to be used effectively.

Having developed and prepared the customer profit and loss account it will become of fundamental importance in the following activities.

1   Assessing comparative profitability.
2   Assessing comparative performance and hence monitoring and controlling the total effort to obtain and maintain business with major customers.
3   Planning major customer strategies and tactics.
4   Allocations of company resources.

Action planning checklist

	Questions	Answers and action	Timing of action and evaluation
1	Up to what level of costs is customer profitability currently calculated? Does this provide sufficient information?		
2	What variable costs and functional expenses are relevant to assessing major customers?		
3	What systems currently exist to generate the necessary information on revenues and costs?		
4	How should the profit and loss format be laid out?		
5	Who currently receives customer profit information and who should receive it?		
6	What training is required to ensure that the correct information is produced and effectively used?		

5
The planning process

5.1 INTRODUCTION

Planning is sometimes heavily criticised by both salesmen and sales management on the grounds that it involves too many restrictions on their activities and that an experienced sales team must be capable of reacting quickly to changes in the market place. These are not criticisms of planning but of bad planning.

The aim of the plan is not to create a strait jacket. It is to make certain that men, money, facilities and time are used to the best advantage. This is of vital importance in obtaining business from major customers, since more often than not a team of people will be involved. Without a detailed plan the problem of co-ordinating their activity would be considerably greater. In addition, without a plan it is difficult to ensure that the correct priorities are allocated or that minor but still important aspects of the company's activities are not overlooked.

The reader will doubtless be familiar with the three parts of the management planning process. This involves the answers to three fundamental questions:

1   Where are we going? (The objective setting process.)
2   How will we get there? (The planning process.)
3   How will we know if we are getting there? (The control process.)

The first two questions are answered in this chapter and the final chapter discusses the third, related to major accounts. It will assist the marketing director in evaluating major customer plans and the salesman and sales manager in developing them. However, it must be emphasised, at this stage, that the answers to the three questions are only meaningful within the company's corporate objectives, corporate plans and corporate control mechanisms. There is little point in setting specific objectives, plans and systems for major customers if the remainder of the sales activity lacks such a mechanism. There is little point in planning sales, if no planning occurs for marketing, production, research and development, finance and for the company as a whole.

With a significant proportion of its business in the hands of relatively few major customers, can any supplier risk not planning in detail to secure this vital revenue? If, in doing so, it stimulates planning activity in other parts of the company where previously it did not occur then the planning will have been doubly beneficial. If it does not, then it will probably soon also cease.

5.2 SETTING OBJECTIVES FOR MAJOR CUSTOMERS

It is generally necessary to set two sets of objectives for the major customer – sales and profit. The responsibility for determining the objectives will be that of the sales/marketing/general manager and salesman most directly concerned. They may carry this out individually or as members of a marketing team. In other cases the forecasts may be prepared by a staff function, such as the marketing services department, although, unless there is an input from those individuals nearest to the particular customer, the validity of these forecasts is always questionable.

Setting sales objectives

Almost by definition each customer is unique. In particular, each major customer differs from all other customers. When forecasting sales for the whole company, or for individual sales territories, this does not matter since the numbers of customers concerned are usually large enough to enable statistical techniques to be used with a reasonable degree of confidence. However, such techniques are much less valid when applied to individual customers. Fortunately, a combination of common sense, intuition and arithmetic usually provides reasonably good forecasts.

It is important to differentiate between three different situations:

1 Sales direct to the user of the product, who orders frequently, each order being relatively small compared to his total purchases from the particular supplier.
2 Sales to a distributor, dealer or wholesaler who, as a member of a distribution channel, will re-sell the product to the final user. The distributor will tend to order frequently from the supplier in order to minimise his stock holding costs.
3 Sales to the user of the product who orders infrequently, perhaps only once or twice per year, each order being relatively large. This is characteristically the case with a capital goods supplier.

Many small orders direct to the user

The forecast is compiled in a number of steps:

1 Tabulate past sales figures.
2 Estimate current year's sales.
3 Identify share of customer's total purchases.
4 Estimate customer's likely purchases next year and forecast sales.
5 Check forecast sales against past sales.

Step 1: tabulate past sales figures

The first stage of forecasting is to look at past sales statistics. The figures shown in Table 5.1 show annual sales to major customer X over the last three years for each of three product ranges in volume terms, together with the total sales revenue.

Table 5.1   Volume and value sales

	Sales volume (tonnes)			Total tonnes	Revenue £
	Product 1	Product 2	Product 3		
3 years ago	50	10	4	64	124,000
2 years ago	55	15	14	84	248,600
1 year ago	52	17	30	99	383,200
Current year to date (9 months)	43	15	30	88	425,900

Examination of the figures in Table 5.1 shows total tonnage sales have increased from 64 tonnes to 99 tonnes, an increase of nearly 55 per cent in volume up to the end of last year. Most of this increase is accounted for by product 3 and some by product 2. Product 1 has remained fairly static. Revenue, on the other hand, has increased dramatically by over 300 per cent in the same three years. This is due to two factors: (a) products 2 and 3 are respectively twice and three times the price per tonne of product 1; (b) all prices have increased each year as a result of inflation.

Therefore, it is apparent that the total revenue figure is of only limited use in making a forecast of next year's sales since it hides many of the details of what is actually happening with the customer. Sales volume is a much better indicator.

Step 2: estimate current year's sales
The next stage is to estimate the likely sales this year before attempting to forecast next year's sales. This can be done by analysing the proportion of sales that fall in each quarter of the year, as shown in Table 5.2, which indicates that on average a quarter of the sales fall in the last quarter of the year.

Table 5.2   Percentage sales per quarter

	Per cent			
	Q1	Q2	Q3	Q4
3 years ago	22	35	15	28
2 years ago	18	38	20	24
1 year ago	20	38	19	23
Average %	20	37	18	25

Thus, it is possible to work out the estimated annual sales for this year by multiplying the nine month figure by $1\frac{1}{3}$. For the purposes of simplification of the example, it has been assumed that each product exhibits similar sales fluctuations in each quarter. If this were not the case, then the above analysis would have to be carried out for each product.

Step 3: identify share of customer's total purchases
The sales figures for the last three years and estimates for this year are shown in Table 5.3, together with the estimated total purchases of each product from all suppliers by customer X.

The top figure in each box is the actual sales by the company to the customer and the bottom one is the estimate of customer X's total purchase from all suppliers of the product. Examination of these figures shows a markedly different picture to that shown by Table 5.1. From the earlier figures it would be easy for management to conclude that overall it was doing very well with this customer, particularly with product 3, although product 1 appeared to have hit a plateau. The latter figures in Table 5.3 show that this is far from the truth. Its total share of customer X's business has remained roughly the same over four years at around 35 per cent. Product 3 has improved its position from less than 4 per cent of the business to over 18 per cent although it clearly has some way to go. Product 2 is slipping from 50 per cent to 40 per cent share. Product 1, on the other hand, the long established breadwinner, is holding on to its nearly 100 per cent share.

Table 5.3 Share of customer purchases

Product	Product sales volume (tonnes)			
	1	2	3	Total
3 years ago	50 / 55	10 / 20	4 / 110	64 / 185
2 years ago	55 / 57	15 / 28	14 / 170	84 / 255
Last year	52 / 52	17 / 35	30 / 200	99 / 287
Current year (estimate)	52 / 59	20 / 50	40 / 220	117 / 329

Before proceeding to make next year's sales forecast, it will be useful to discuss how the total purchases figures from all suppliers is obtained. There is no standard or correct way of doing this; it is merely a process of piecing together separate pieces of information, gathered in many different ways, including the following.

1 Asking the buyer, factory manager or engineer.
2 Identifying customer X's sales of associated products. For example, if the supplier knows that his products are used as a component to produce, say, a printing machine, then he need only get an estimate of the total number of printing machines produced or sold by the customer to estimate his total purchases.
3 Stock checks of the customer's inventory and asking the storekeeper.
4 Providing customer with inventory control systems preferably linked in with the supplier's computer.
5 Discussions with competitive suppliers.

None of these ways will give completely accurate figures, although some will be more reliable than others, depending on individual circumstances.

Step 4: estimate customer's likely purchases next year and forecast sales
To produce next year's sales forecast it is necessary to estimate the customer's total purchases. Again some of the methods suggested above can be used. It is necessary to relate these to one's own knowledge of the market in which the customer is operating. Then an estimate can be made of the amount by which total purchases will increase or decline or remain static. Table 5.4 shows these estimates, together with the sales forecast for next year.

Table 5.4 Supplier and customer sales forecast

	Product sales volume			
	1	2	3	Total
Next year – own sales	58	25	58	141
Total customer purchases	60	65	250	375

Next it is necessary to adjust the forecast figures in the light of other factors that are likely to have an effect next year. In particular, note should be taken of what will differ next year compared with this and previous years. For example, if the supplier is looking for substantially increased sales to be brought about by trade exhibitions, reorganisation of the sales effort and improved customer service then the figures, particularly for product 3, may be revised upwards. Conversely, if competitive pressures are expected to increase with a new supplier entering the market then the estimates may be revised downwards.

Step 5: check forecast sales against past sales
Since the past is often a good guide as to what will happen in the future, it is wise to plot these sales forecasts and actual past sales graphically as shown in Figure 5.1. From this review the manager might question the forecasts for products 1 and 3. The former is expected to reach a slightly higher level than ever before, whilst the latter is growing faster than previously. This will encourage further detailed examination and justification of the forecast. If sufficient justification cannot be found then the forecast should be amended.

Finally, it is necessary to calculate sterling sales, bearing in mind likely price increases. Where a company sells a very wide product range the method using sales volume may prove somewhat impractical and revenue figures may be the only ones conveniently available. If this is the case then every effort should be made to assess the effect of price increases and significant changes in sales mix using some form of price indexing. The forecasts should then be made on the basis discussed above, i.e. as a proportion of the customer's total projected purchases for the product group.

Where the customer operates from a number of locations, each representing a different buying and delivery point, although co-ordinated and controlled by the centre, then greater accuracy will be obtained if sales forecasts are made for each buying point or geographic area and the individual parts totalled to give a total customer sales forecast. Similarly, when each product is used for a number of applications, forecasts should be made for each application.

Many small orders to a distributor
This differs from the preceding case in that the customer is likely to buy a wide range of products and sizes for resale, making difficult both individual product forecasting and estimating the share of customer total purchases.

Methods used in the previous case can be used here with more emphasis being placed on:

(a) stock audits;
(b) closer integration with the distributor;
(c) forecasting the final user market for the products.

Stock audits are prevalent in the fast moving consumer goods business with A.C. Nielsen, Stats M R and similar organisations conducting store audits. Closer integration occurs in such sectors as the motor vehicle industry and agricultural equipment where the manufacturers will support their distributors by providing management systems, training and marketing help. The forecasting of the user market lends itself to quantitative techniques and is usually the province of the marketing department who should provide the necessary guidelines. In making the forecast the supplier must take into account factors which will affect the customer's total purchases such as market growth and new outlet openings, and those factors which will affect his share of that business such as sales effort, new products and advertising.

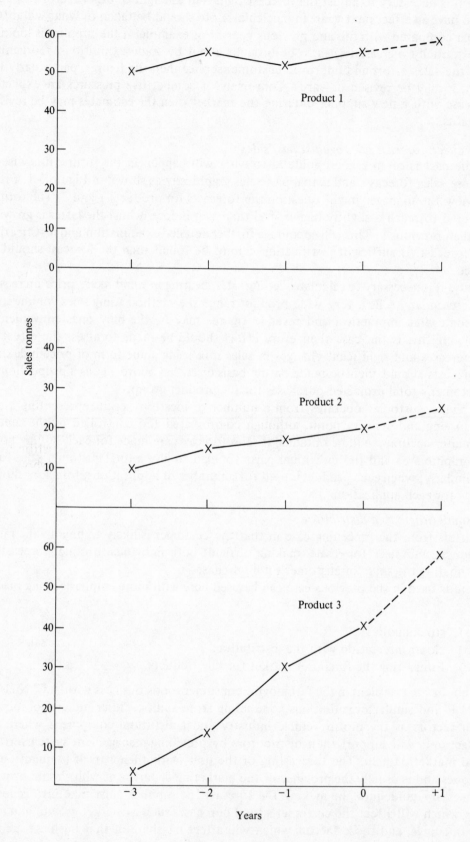

Figure 5.1   Graphical representation of sales forecasts

The capital goods buyer
Frequently the capital goods purchase is characterised by the following factors.

1 The lead time is long, months and even years between initial enquiry and the placing of the order.
2 The value of the order is large, many thousands or even millions of pounds.
3 Each major customer tends to order relatively infrequently.

These factors make sales forecasting very difficult since the supplier is attempting to predict unique events. Often it is not so much the value of the order which has to be forecast (since this will have been determined in the original quotation) as its timing.

From experience salesmen are often optimistic about the arrival of a big order. Such optimism even extends to government ministers when announcing a large overseas deal before all the details have been settled.

The problems in making an accurate forecast of timing present difficulties for the effective organisation of production, design and engineering facilities. To help overcome such problems, and increase the degree of planning and control in the business, the following approach has proved useful.

1 Divide the year into four quarters.
2 Estimate the quarter within which the order is most likely to fall, together with the probability of this occurring.
3 Estimate the probability of the order landing in the preceding and succeeding quarters.
4 Where the lead times are long, or the probabilities very uncertain, then it may be necessary to extend the projection over two or more years.

Generally the sales representative and sales/marketing manager will be in the best position to make these estimates. Thus, the following two questions need to be answered.

1 What is the probability of getting the order?
2 Assuming the order is obtained, what is the probability of its landing in a particular quarter?

The figures in Table 5.5 show how these calculations may be made for three large customers with whom quotations of £1m, £2m and £3m respectively are outstanding.

Table 5.5   Expected value of order input

	Order size (a)	Probability of obtaining the order (b)	Conditional probability of obtaining the order in each quarter (c)				Expected value per quarter £m (a × b × c)			
	£m	P	Q1	Q2	Q3	Q4	Q1	Q2	Q3	Q4
Customer 1	1	0.8	–	–	0.5	0.5	–	–	0.4	0.4
2	2	0.5	0.1	0.7	0.2	–	0.1	0.7	0.2	–
3	3	0.7	–	0.6	0.2	0.2	–	1.3	0.4	0.4

If there are sufficiently large numbers of prospective big orders (generally ten or more) then the additions of the expected order value columns will give a reasonably accurate picture of likely order input in each quarter.

For the individual large customer the analysis gives some concept of when the order is likely to come and the possible variance, together with the likelihood of obtaining the order anyway. This will enable a judgement to be made of the effort required to ensure the order is forthcoming, or at least increase the probability of it occurring. Additionally, it will facilitate the control of the total effort directed to the customer.

Setting the profit objective

Having set the sales objectives for the major customer it will then be possible to determine the profit objective. For the capital plant customer this will have been done during the initial quotation stage. The supplier's skill and experience is devoted to making certain that this profit margin is achieved during the fulfilment of the subsequent contract.

The other type of user customer (many small orders) and the distributor type customer can also usefully have profit objectives set. These must be related, in part, to the overall company profit objectives. A profit and loss format that provides a convenient means for determining the profit objectives is shown in Table 5.6.

Table 5.6   Contribution and trading profit

CUSTOMER ....X....................................

		This year actual		Initial projection Next year plan	
		£000s Total	% Total income	£000s Total	% Total income
1	Gross sales value	569	93.1	884	93.1
2	Service revenue	34	5.6	57	6.0
3	Other revenue	8	1.3	9	0.9
4	Total income	611	100	950	100
5	Less: Invoiced discounts	71	11.6	100	10.6
6	Net income	540	88.4	850	89.4
7	Less: Manufacturing costs	272	44.5	438	46.1
8	Customer gross profit	268	43.9	412	43.3
9	Less: Special price allowances	4	0.7	5	0.5
10	: Direct transport costs	7?	11.8	112	11.8
11	: Trade-in allowances	4?	7.8	69	7.3
12	: Direct sales force costs	75	12.3	117	12.3
13	: Direct service costs	37	6.0	57	6.0
14	: Direct training costs	24	3.9	36	3.8
15	: Direct promotion cost	6	1.0	5	0.5
16	: Direct entertaining cost	1	0.2	1	0.1
17	Customer contribution	1	0.2	10	1.0
18	Less: Outstanding debt interest	4	0.7	7	0.7
19	: Stock interest	7	1.1	10	1.1
20	Trading profit (loss)	(10)	(1.6)	(7)	(0.8)
21	Less: Overhead allocations				
22	: Sales	40	6.5	62	6.5
23	: Marketing	20	3.3	31	3.3
24	: Service	35	5.7	54	5.7
25	: Distribution	27	4.4	42	4.4
26	: General and administration	7	1.1	11	1.1
27	Net profit	(139)	(22.6)	(207)	(21.8)

Returning to the earlier example of the supplier selling three products (1, 2 and 3) the sales projections yield a gross sales revenue value of £884,000 for customer X. This takes account of an expected overall price increase of 20 per cent in the forthcoming year. A review of 'this year's' results shown in the first two columns of Table 5.6 shows that this customer is trading at a loss of around 1.6 per cent (line 20) of total income (line 4). Management, in looking into next year, is concerned that this loss should be reduced and if possible would like to eliminate it. To assess the feasibility of doing so, each cost element needs to be examined to identify how it is likely to change, if at all, next year. A number of projections will have to be made, with management deciding when a satisfactory position has been reached. The second two columns in Table 5.6 show the first set of projections made for next year, which are likely to be subject to further modifications after being reviewed.

The main difficulty about increasing the trading profit is the relative increase in manufacturing costs (line 7) from 44.5 per cent to 46.1 per cent. This has arisen in this case because the manufacturing costs of products 2 and 3 are considerably higher than product 1 and, although they sell at higher prices, the gross margins are less than those available on product 1 because of the increased competitive situation. Thus, although sales revenue has increased dramatically, the cost structure has not enabled gross profit to increase parallel with it. Unless a profitability analysis is carried out for each customer this information will never be highlighted and the sales manager might be quite happy to give increased discounts, credit or trade-in allowances, feeling that an increase of over 55 per cent in sales revenue must surely cover these minimal concessions.

In the initial projection, the account sales executive has identified areas where he feels some savings can be made. There is some scope for reductions in invoiced discounts (line 5) since these have been based on the gross margins available on product 1 and do not take into account the lower margins on products 2 and 3. Likewise a reduction in price allowances (line 9) and trade-in allowances (line 11) is feasible. All other costs remain constant except promotion and entertaining costs (lines 15 and 16) which have been halved.

The effect of these savings is to increase the customer contribution (line 17) significantly to £10,000 and reduce the trading loss (line 20) from £10,000 to £7,000. Should management not be satisfied with this trading loss objective then further consideration is required and additional projections must be made.

Other areas where savings might be possible are in sales force and service costs (lines 12 and 13). However, if the major account sales manager feels that an increase rather than a decrease in sales effort is required to generate the sales forecast, then the scope for decreasing sales costs might be limited.

It is apparent, therefore, that with each projection an even more detailed examination of costs and revenues is required to assess where additional scope exists, if any, to reduce costs and increase revenues.

The sales forecasting and profit planning activity is thus a two-way process. The initial forecasts are made, reviewed, and assessed against the desired profit objectives. If all is satisfactory then sales management can proceed with its detailed planning activity. However, if the projected profit objectives are not in line with company requirements then the sales and costs projections need to be reviewed again. This process continues in an iterative manner until a satisfactory state is obtained. The amount of change between the initial projection and the final agreed sales and profit forecast should be relatively small. The two-way process is essentially one of 'fine tuning'. If large changes are necessary then the overall objectives may be unrealistic or fundamental errors may have been made in forecasting and further investigation is required. As a result it will be necessary either to refine the overall objectives set by senior management or to provide training for the staff who do the major customer planning.

5.3   DEVELOPING MAJOR ACCOUNT PLANS

Having set the sales and profit objectives it is then necessary to draw up detailed plans for each major customer. This can best be tackled in two stages:

Stage 1: Qualitative analysis of the company's offering to the customer.
Stage 2: Development of an account strategy and action plan.

If the plans are to be most useful they must be judged against five criteria. They should be:

(a)   specific, listing particular detailed activity;
(b)   easily measured, quantified whenever possible;
(c)   succinct, easily read and understood by those involved and responsible;
(d)   directive, showing clearly what is required from each individual or department concerned;
(e)   basis for commitment, by the individuals to the achievement of the objectives.

Stage 1: qualitative analysis

The purpose of this stage is to evaluate the quality of the company's offering to the customer. This will enable the *value* to both parties to be determined. As a result an extra dimension is added to the quantitative picture of sales and profit which will be required to determine an effective strategy to achieve the objectives.

A simple format, to assist in this analysis, is to divide the company's offering into three main component parts: (a) product, (b) price and terms, (c) presentation, and assess them against the competition. In particular it is necessary to look at the areas where buying influence exists within the customer's operation to review the position in comparison with the competition.

The depth of analysis will vary from product to product and customer to customer, but the aim is to identify strengths and weaknesses compared to competition as seen from the customer's point of view. In Table 5.7 a convenient format is presented for comparing the product, price and presentation with that of competitors.

The particular product in the example is an industrial one, sold to manufacturing industry. It is a component used by the customer to fit into a consumer durable for retail sale. There is only one competitor in this case, but if there were more, each one would require an additional line. There are five influences on the buying decision – the design/production planning department, the purchasing department, the production department, the marketing department and the final customer who buys the output of the company to whom the supplier is directing his effort.

The nature of the influence which each department will exert will vary with their area of responsibility and individual needs. For the large customer it is often worthwhile for the salesman, or whoever else in the team is closest to the relevant individual, to sketch a cameo of the most influential personnel in each department. This will facilitate the exercise of looking at ourselves from the customer's point of view.

The first line in Table 5.7, our product, shows how each of the four departments and the final customer view the product offering. In particular the design department is concerned that any product meets the laid down technical specification. The second line, competitor's product, reviews the product offering of the competitor. In the case of design department the exact specification is not met by the competitor although it is fairly close, the difference being a matter of small detail.

Table 5.7   Competitor comparison format

| | Customer buying influences | | | | |
	Design	Purchasing	Production	Marketing	Customer's customer
Our product	Meets specification	Not previously purchased. 12 month guarantee and 24 hour spares service	Easy to dismantle and fit	Enables delivery promises to be kept	Meets all standard uses
Competitor's product	Specification will need slight modification	Previously purchased. 18 month guarantee and no promise on spares	Difficult to fit and service	Allows a greater number of end product extras to be incorporated	Slightly greater variety of uses for end product
Our price	Acceptable	High	Little high	Slight increase in finished product price	NA
Competitor's price	Acceptable	15% lower	Acceptable	Acceptable	NA
Our presentation	Very good – stresses reliability	Good – stresses reliability	Frequent sales visit and named inside sales contact	NA	Well-known company name
Competitor's presentation	Good – stresses versatility	Very good – stresses price	Has large stand at all trade exhibitions	NA	Less well known

For the buying department the key factor is whether the product has been bought previously and they have had experience of the supplier. The second important factor is a good spares service since they re-sell the components to the public at a large profit. Our product has not previously been purchased whereas the competitor's product has. The guarantee on our product is 12 months compared to 18 months for the competitor. This can work to our advantage since lucrative replacement sales can start more quickly for the customer providing we can maintain availability of spares to within a reliable 24 hours.

The production department is primarily concerned with producing as many units as it can, whilst not exceeding budgeted costs. Thus, the fact that our product is easy to dismantle and fit, compared to the competitive offering, will reduce standard production times and hence costs.

The marketing department's main requirement is to make sure it has a good looking and reasonably reliable product to offer at all times to meet customer demand. Because of our service we can offer continuity of supply. We know the competition has been experiencing slight delivery problems but the nature of their product offering enables a greater number of optional extras to be included which gives this customer an edge over its competitors.

As far as the final user is concerned he rarely sees our product since it is built into the machine. However, the capacity of our product is such that it will efficiently cater for all standard uses. The competitor's product will allow a slightly greater variety of uses linked to additional optional extras.

A similar exercise is carried out for price and presentation. In looking at price the supplier is aware that it will be of varying importance to the different departments. Not only price but the total terms of business should be compared. The purchasing department is likely to make much of any adverse price situation, the production department much less so with any difference being overcome by ease of fitting the component. Marketing is concerned only with the price of the finished product.

The term presentation refers to all the other factors associated with the supplier's offering besides the product itself and price. It includes packaging, sales force, advertising, exhibition and promotions, research and development support, applications support, design facility, company image and so on. In consumer products and service companies any of these factors might be sufficiently important to warrant a separate heading. For example, the large soap companies such as Procter and Gamble, Unilever and Colgate Palmolive might wish to do a detailed breakdown of advertising effort as this is one of the key variables. A computer peripheral supplies company might want to include the type of sales effort it possesses since this is a key factor in determining sales.

Often a supplier tends to be most subjective in assessing how good his presentation is. A particular case is a farm equipment supplier who, when asked, felt he sold a 'Rolls Royce' type product. Unfortunately, the dealers and farmers only perceived a 'Ford' at a 'Rolls Royce' price. Clearly outside help may be required to obtain more objective information.

For the industrial component example in Table 5.7 the customer will tend to be much more objective although not completely so. The design department, for example, is concerned that the finished product should work during the guarantee period (1 year) and this need will be satisfied by the fact that our product literature stresses reliability.

The production department is responsible for the non-stop working of the production line, and frequent contact by the supplier's sales engineer and internal desk sales staff is felt to be advantageous over the competitor who does not have a named internal sales contact for this major customer. The presentation is of little applicability to the marketing department hence NA (not applicable).

Stage 2: developing the individual major customer plan

Setting objectives and carrying out the qualitative analysis provide the bedrock upon which a strategy for each major customer can be developed. Such a strategy is developed by answering the fundamental question: 'What do I have to do better than my competitors to achieve the sales and profit objectives for this customer?'

There are a multitude of possible answers depending on the market, the competitive situation and the customer, and the supplier's resources. In one case, as with a supplier of capital goods to the metal manufacturing industries, all the supplier had to do was make sure his product did the job it was supposed to do and he would be almost certain to get sufficient repeat orders to achieve his objectives.

For a grocery company it often boils down to making certain that a planned number of promotions are achieved with a multiple grocery company, at the *right* price, with sufficient in-store support to shift the product off the shelves and reduce the competitor's market share.

An industrial supplies company selling to manufacturing industry needed to ensure that the large customer sales engineer had detailed applications knowledge, applied the sales training he had learned and used the technical and senior management resources available to him. For a service company 'supplying industry' it was a question of maintaining the quality of the service to its major customers and increasing the senior management contact in another division of the customer.

The definition of the major account strategy will provide the framework for the main tactical activities that will take place during next year to achieve the objectives of the major customer. The nature and scale of these tactical activities, some of which are given in Table 5.8, will vary from business to business.

Table 5.8   Main tactical variables available to supplier

Frequency of salesman calls	Product modification
Level of sales activity	Research and development, application
Type of sales activity	development
Service levels	Market research
Methods of delivery	Promotional activity
Packaging	Exhibitions
Price	Free trial/sampling
Terms of payment	Sales literature/proposals
Local or customer advertising	Technical support
Training and other forms of customer support	

It is apparent that the development and compilation of a major account plan is a complex matter. The marketing or sales director, however, will have no wish to be bombarded with a lengthy and weighty document for each major customer. To simplify presentation and communication of the plans a standard format should be used which highlights the most important elements of the plan as shown in Figure 5.2. Here the form is condensed to two pages but will generally be at least three pages long. It needs to be tailored by each company to suit their particular circumstances.

The matrix format provides a useful method of summarising the main information. This in no way replaces the need for the detailed analysis and forecasting discussed above, but is merely a convenient way of summarising the results of such an analysis. Further refinements can be added such as specifically summarising the main activities to be carried out by each department, or a monthly or quarterly sales breakdown.

Finally it is necessary to cost all the activities to make certain that the required customer profitability objectives are still being achieved. If they are not then the plan needs to be reformulated and re-costed.

Two examples are shown in Figures 5.3 and 5.4 relating to a consumer goods and industrial products company respectively.

5.4 COMPILATION OF PLANS

The compilation of major customer plans is generally done by the sales manager or account executive most closely associated with the customer. However, he cannot carry out this activity in isolation, since, as discussed earlier, a number of other people are likely to be involved with the customer such as the salesman, application engineer, sales/marketing director, design staff and internal salesman.

It is vital that all those involved contribute to the formulation of the plan. This will be trebly beneficial in the following ways.

1   Production of a better plan since all relevant information will be included.
2   Increasing the commitment of all staff to implementing the plan.
3   Providing a mechanism for communications amongst the group.

Customer name and address _____

_____

_____

Date of compilation _____   Period covered by plan: _____

Staff currently servicing this customer   Customer contacts

Name	Department	Name	Position
_____	_____	_____	_____
_____	_____	_____	_____
_____	_____	_____	_____
_____	_____	_____	_____
_____	_____	_____	_____

This year

		Applications/markets/locations			Trend	Total
		(a)	(b)	(c)		
P R O D U C T S	A	Potential Actual				
	B	P A				
	C	P A				
	D	P A				
Trend						
Total		P A				

Competitive activity _____

_____

Objectives for next year

1   Sales

		Applications/markets/locations			Total
		(a)	(b)	(c)	
P R O D U C T S	A	Potential Actual			
	B	P A			
	C	P A			
	D	P A			
Total					

Figure 5.2   Major customer plan form

2 Profit		This year		Next year	
		£	%	£	%
Gross sales Invoiced discounts Net income					
Manufacturing costs Customer gross profit					
Price allowances Delivery costs Sales force costs Promotion cost Customer contribution					
Debt interest Stock interest Trading profit					
Overhead allocations Net profit					

Plan for next year

Customer strategy statement

_____

_____

_____

Activity plan and timing

_____

_____

_____

Sales

_____

_____

_____

Marketing

_____

_____

_____

Support functions

_____

_____

_____

Compilation of plan co-ordinated by: _____

Figure 5.2 (continued)

Customer name
and address

Head Office
Electronic Chain Stores Ltd
High Street
London
Tel: 01-935 3330
Branches throughout Great Britain

Date of compilation: 31 October 1978

Period covered by plan: 1979

Staff currently servicing this customer

Customer contacts

Name	Department	Name	Position
J. Smith	National accounts dept	L. Brown	Purchasing director
All salesmen	Sales	S. Black	Merchandising manager
P. Muire	Marketing	D. Jones	Regional controller south
			All store managers and many assistants

This year

Projections up to year end – units

			South	Midlands	North	Trend	Total
Number of sets	Products	Black and white	P 2,000 A 1,000	1,500 500	1,200 300	Declining	4,700 1,800
		Colour	P 1,500 A 800	2,000 800	1,500 400	Static	5,000 2,000
		Hi-Fi	P 1,000 A 300	500 100	400 100	Expanding more slowly	1,900 500
		Trend	Decreasing	Static	Increasing		
		Total	P 4,500 A 2,100	4,000 1,400	3,100 800		11,600 4,300

Locations (column span over South, Midlands, North)

Competitive activity

Competition relatively strong in Midlands and North regions because of traditional ties with local factories. Product competition is heavy particularly on black and white and to a lesser degree on colour sets. Competitor Y is beginning to promote heavily in the North. South slowly establishing reputation for Hi-Fi.

Objectives next year

1   *Sales – units*

			South	Midlands	North	Total
Number of sets	Products	Black and white	P 1,800 A 1,200	1,400 500	1,150 400	4,350 2,100
		Colour	P 1,400 A 1,000	2,200 800	1,400 500	5,000 2,300
		Hi-Fi	P 1,100 A 400	550 150	450 120	2,100 670
		Total	P 4,300 A 2,600	4,150 1,450	3,000 1,020	11,450 5,070

Locations (column span over South, Midlands, North)

Figure 5.3:   Major customer plan form. Consumer goods example: electrical goods. P = potential, A = actual.

2   *Profit*

	This year		Next year	
	£000s	%	£	%
Gross sales (trade list)	412	100	524	100
Invoiced discounts	78	18.9	99	18.9
Net income	334	81.1	425	81.1
Manufacturing costs	223	54.1	283	54.0
Customer gross profit	111	27.0	142	27.1
Price allowances and overriders	25	6.1	39	7.5
Direct delivery transportation costs	33	8.0	10	2.0
Direct sales force costs	23	5.6	21	4.0
Direct promotional costs	35	8.5	49	9.3
Customer contribution	(5)	(1.2)	23	4.3
Debt interest	3	0.7	4	0.7
Stock interest	6	1.5	5	1.0
Trading profit (loss)	(14)	(3.4)	14	2.6
Overhead allocation	35	8.5	52	10.0
Net profit (loss)	(49)	(11.9)	(38)	(7.4)

Plan for next year

Strategy statement

To increase sales it is necessary to penetrate further into the Midlands and North and maintain the competitive advantage in the South. To achieve the profit objective it is imperative that we move to central depot delivery, as opposed to branch delivery currently, and reduce the frequency of branch calling by the sales staff. This will be offset by increased allowances, promotional activity and the major national advertising campaign planned for next year.

Activity plan
   Sales

Contacts to be made. Each region is virtually autonomous for buying purposes under general policy guidance of purchasing director. Must make contact therefore with regional controllers for Midlands and North. Warehousing and distribution controllers to be contacted.

Call frequency. Recommend maintenance of four-weekly cycle to central buying and eight-weekly contact with merchandising to arrange special display, etc. Monthly visit to HO.

Objectives of call:

   1   To negotiate central delivery by 1 February and ensure system operates smoothly.
   2   To ensure Midlands and North controllers fully aware of our product range, pricing structure and after sales service. Establish first contact by 1 March.
   3   We arrange at least four special promotions of our range during the year. One per quarter.
   4   To arrange contract purchasing of colour sets by 1 July.

   Marketing

1   Brand managers to make presentation to purchasing director, merchandising manager, regional controllers and distribution controller on advertising, promotional and development activity planned for the year, by end February.
2   Marketing director to assist in central delivery negotiations, ASAP.
3   Specific, tailor made in-store promotional material to be supplied by end March.

   Support functions

1   Distribution to give detailed delivery cost breakdown to assist in negotiations – ASAP.
2   Finance to advise on better contract arrangements for colour sets – end March.
3   Warehousing to reduce stock for this customer to six weeks but earmark it – 1 March.

Compilation of plan co-ordinated by L. Pearce, National Accounts Manager.

Figure 5.3 (continued)

Customer name and address

XYZ Bottlers Company Ltd
Main Street
Newtown
Tel: Newtown 123

Date of compilation: 31 August 1978   Period covered by plan: financial year 1978/9

Staff currently servicing this customer   Customer contacts

Name	Department	Name	Position
G. Holland	Sales	F. Smith	Assistant buyer
P. Stoll	Desk sales	J. Jenkins	Works manager
All progress clerks	Prod'n planning	L. Peters	Assistant brand
J. White	Marketing		manager
L. Palmer	Technical support		

This year

			Applications			
		Gin	Whisky	Vodka	Trend	Total
Number of units in grosses	Products — Miniature	P 1,000 A 600	5,000 3,000	? 500	Increasing because of airline business	6,000 + ? 4,100
	Half bottle (375 ml)	P10,000 A 5,000	20,000 12,000	? 500	Static	30,000 + ? 17,500
	Bottle (750 ml)	P25,000 A 5,000	50,000 18,000	? 500	Decreasing because of tax and price increases	75,000 + ? 23,500
Trend		Static	Slightly increasing	New line seems to be increasing		
Total		36,000 10,600	75,000 33,000	? 1,500		111,000 + ? 45,100

Competitive activity

Competition very strong in 750 ml bottles because of price. Also trying to attack our miniature bottle sales.
Traditionally this customer has sourced mainly from company P. Due to supply problems they are now buying in
Europe and from wholesalers.

1   *Sales – units*   *Objectives next year*

		Gin	Whisky	Vodka	Total
Products	Miniature	P 1,000 A 700	5,500 4,000	? 550	6,500 + ? 5,250
	Half bottle (375 ml)	P10,000 A 6,000	21,000 15,000	? 550	31,000 + ? 21,550
	Bottle (750 ml)	P25,000 A10,000	55,000 25,000	? 550	80,000 + ? 35,550
	Total	36,000 16,700	81,500 44,000	? 1,650	117,500 + ? 62,350

Figure 5.4   Major customer plan form
Industrial example: glass containers. P = potential, A = actual.

2   *Profit*

	This year		Next year	
	£000s	%	£000s	%
Gross sales value	825	100	902	100
Invoiced discounts	91	11.0	99	11.0
Net sales	734	89.0	803	89.0
Manufacturing costs	536	65.0	586	65.0
Distribution costs	91	11.0	99	11.0
Customer gross profit	107	13.0	118	13.0
Direct outside sales cost	17	2.1	16	1.7
Direct inside sales cost	24	2.9	25	2.8
Direct technical support	13	1.6	15	1.7
Customer contribution	53	6.4	62	6.8
Debt interest	2	0.2	1	0.1
Stock interest	3	0.4	4	0.4
Trading profit (loss)	48	5.8	57	6.3
Overhead allocation	45	5.5	50	5.5
Net profit (loss)	3	0.3	7	0.8

Plans for next year

Strategy statement

The main task for next year is to integrate ourselves more closely with this customer and obtain increased knowledge about him. The main sales increases will come from the 750 ml container where it is expected that substitution of the European source will take place. Profits will increase by reducing debtors from two months to six weeks and slightly reducing the frequency of call. However, more time will be spent on each call and technical support will be increased.

Activity plan
    Sales

Contacts to be made:
1   Must establish contact with chief buyer as he handles vodka line where we have little information – 31 January.
2   Must also contact marketing department to try to establish brand plans – end December.
3   Suspect company will put strong effort behind vodka, and ease off gin – end December.

Call frequency:
1   Need to reduce to every four weeks except in pre-Christmas period when every two weeks – ASAP.
2   Increase time spent to three hours average per call – ASAP.

Objectives of call:
1   To identify size of vodka business and future intentions.
2   To stress our technical expertise to combat price competition.
3   To increase gin business by indicating better bulk discounts on slightly larger order.
4   To increase whisky business by offering stock back-up.

    Technical support

1   Visit production facility of customer monthly by March.
2   Investigate possibility of special closure on 750 ml – end October.

    Support functions

1   Arrange visit to our manufacturing plant – end January.
2   Introduce sales director to chief buyer and his production director.
3   Market research department to supply any information available on vodka market – end December.
4   Distribution and finance controllers to sanction increase in 750 ml back-up stock to facilitate faster delivery.

Compilation of plan co-ordinated by T. Crow, Technical Sales Representative.

Figure 5.4 (continued)

Whether a team meeting is called or the sales manager holds individual discussions, based on pre-circulated documents, depends on the particular organisation. However, it is imperative that difficulties in contacting individuals should not be used as an excuse for them to be excluded from planning; major customers are too important.

Having developed the plans within the guidelines laid down by senior management the account executive must agree the plans with his manager. This planning meeting will provide the basis of the account executive's activity during the following year and the yardstick against which his performance will be judged.

5.5 SUMMARY

This chapter has described the steps needed to develop major account plans, a process which is carried out once a year and involves the following:

1 Forecasting sales and profit objectives.
2 Analysing strengths and weaknesses of the 'offering' in the customer's eyes.
3 Developing a major account strategy.
4 Identifying the main activities to be carried out to ensure that the objectives are achieved.
5 Completing a major customer plan form for each major customer to be presented to, and agreed by, senior management.

Unless meaningful plans are drawn up the activity towards large customers will tend to become unco-ordinated and the results achieved less than optimal. Experience has shown that those companies who carry out the planning activity effectively mobilise their resources efficiently, maximise the profits they achieve and have a mutually rewarding relationship with their major customers.

For the plans to make maximum impact they should be

(a) specific, listing detailed activity;
(b) easily measured, quantified whenever possible;
(c) succinct, easily read and understood by those involved and responsible;
(d) directive, showing clearly what is required from each individual or department concerned;
(e) a basis for commitment, by the individuals, to the achievement of the objectives.

Action planning checklist

Questions	Answers and action	Timing of action and evaluation
1 How are sales to major customers currently forecast and how should this be improved?		
2 What major customer plan format is required?		
3 Are explicit plans currently prepared and how do they compare with the criteria listed?		
4 How does the planning process currently operate and who else should be involved?		
5 What training is required to ensure that the necessary staff: (a) understand the planning format? (b) can forecast realistically? (c) can develop strategy? (d) can develop statements? (e) can plan tactics effectively?		

6
Obtaining customer information

6.1 INTRODUCTION

Obtaining business from, and servicing, large accounts is a complex activity involving numbers of different individuals within the organisation. The effectiveness with which these people operate, assuming they are organised correctly, depends upon how plentiful, how relevant, and how good the information is that they have available and how well it is interpreted and acted upon.

This chapter looks at the information required to plan and implement the approach to individual major customers, and discusses some ways of obtaining this information. In doing so there is often a tendency to ask for more and more information in the belief that it will substantially improve the decisions made. Experience shows that this often leads to 'statistical indigestion'.

The chapter discusses first the problem of obtaining customer intelligence and then that of conducting customer research.

6.2 OBTAINING CUSTOMER INTELLIGENCE

This covers the way in which the relevant executives are kept up to date with changing conditions within the customer. Typically, this occurs in a fairly haphazard and random manner with the staff concerned keeping abreast by talking to customer's personnel, reading newspapers and trade publications, talking to other company personnel and receiving unsolicited information.

Often a supplier may learn much too late that a competitor is trying to win an established major customer from him and have no option left, due to a shortage of time, but to compete on a price basis. Even if he holds the business, it will be at the cost of reduced profitability.

What intelligence should be obtained?

However theoretically desirable it may be to know *everything* that is happening within a customer at all times, this is both impractical and prohibitively costly. It is therefore important to specify what information is *essential*, *desirable* or merely of *interest*. The information system should concentrate on obtaining the essential information, cover as much of the desirable information as can easily be obtained and pick up some of the interesting information in passing.

Essential information will vary from company to company and industry to industry but will almost certainly include:

1   Nature of business and location of sites.
2   Names, positions and locations of key customer staff.
3   Role, authority and idiosyncrasies of key customer staff.

4 Customer sales by product.
5 Relevant ownership of machines or products currently used.
6 Competitive activity; who they are and what part of the customer's business they hold.
7 Financial and credit status.

Further information applicable to particular types of industries includes:

(a) expansion plans;
(b) level and power of unionisation within customer;
(c) new product activity;
(d) international activity;
(e) staff relationship policy;
(f) organisation structure.

Generally when setting up a formal customer intelligence system it is necessary to establish how much additional information is required over and above that which is already known. A convenient matrix format for assessing this is the major customer information audit form shown in Figure 6.1.

Customer name:	Allweather Knitwear Ltd						
	Locations/divisions/companies						
Information requirements	A	B	C	D	E	F	G
Nature of business	✓	✓	✓	✓	✓	✓	
Address	✓	✓	✓	✓		✓	✓
Telephone number	✓		✓			✓	
Key customer's staff:							
Names	✓	✓				✓	
Peculiarities	✓	✓				✓	
Customer's product sales	✓	✓			✓	✓	
Organisation structure	✓		✓			✓	
Competitors	✓					✓	
Share of business						✓	
Level of buying authority			✓			✓	
Employee relations	✓		✓			✓	
Future plans	✓	✓				✓	

The appropriate box is ticked when the information is available. The blank boxes show what further information is required. In this way, management can continually monitor the information still outstanding.

Figure 6.1   Matrix format to establish additional customer information needs. Major customer information audit.

Such information is important but it will only be of real value if it is continually updated. Often it is the fact that there is a change that provides an opportunity or creates a problem. Unless these changes are notified speedily to the right people it may be difficult to rectify the problem or take advantage of the opportunity. In nearly all cases the supplier will have no difficulty in keeping himself aware of the major changes which are occurring within his large customers such as mergers, expansion, changes in buying policy and product quality problems. Often there are many minor changes which, if known about, would be very useful and which existing systems often fail to highlight. For example, the occasion of the retirement of a works director was capitalised on by a supplier of consumables used in the production process by the giving of a small gift to express their thanks for a mutually beneficial business relationship and their wishes for a happy retirement. In fact, they had only ever managed to get a small share of the potential business because the works director had been very loyal to a competitive supplier. The gesture was noted by the new works director and provided a friendly basis to commence a new and, for the supplier, a potentially more lucrative relationship.

Conversely, the recognition of a union for collective bargaining purposes posed a severe problem for a supplier of an on-site maintenance service to engineering manufacturing companies. This came about because the prime benefit of using the service to the customer was cost saving, most of which occurred through savings in labour costs in the maintenance department. Clearly the union would not be serving the interests of its members if it allowed maintenance jobs to go unfilled or if its members were unable to benefit from expansion opportunities. Further, it would considerably reduce the bargaining power of the maintenance men if an outside supplier was involved. Had the supplier not known about the impending unionisation he would have been unable to take avoiding action, and would have lost the business.

Methods of obtaining intelligence

The main source of the intelligence is the salesman and, to a lesser extent, other employees visiting the customer such as service staff, installation engineers and delivery drivers. These people are in a good position to pick up information which never appears in the summary statistics of the sales activity. Such pieces of information when brought together can often reveal a very meaningful picture of the changes that are taking place within the customer.

For this process to occur effectively, it is necessary that the staff concerned feel motivated to identify the relevant information and then to communicate it back in a correct and understandable way. Unfortunately, quite often the salesman is not sufficiently motivated, and it is rare for the other staff calling on the customer to even think of looking for the necessary information. This clearly represents a considerable missed opportunity. One of the reasons this happens is that the various individuals do not see it as part of their role to carry out these functions. Another, and perhaps less excusable reason, is that management appears to fail to respond to the information supplied and hence the employee becomes discouraged from supplying further facts. As a result, significant pieces of information may never be uncovered, or may reach the appropriate decision maker much too late.

The solution lies partly in organisation structure, partly in training and partly in systems. The organisational aspects have been discussed in preceding chapters. Clearly, the greater the commitment of the individual to the effective servicing of the major customer, the higher will be his motivation to accept intelligence gathering as part of his role and the greater the likelihood of his carrying it out.

The intelligence role should be further emphasised by training. In particular, each individual must be made aware of what information is essential, why it is so, how it will be used and most importantly how it will benefit *him* and the company. It has been known for companies to offer some small incentive for obtaining this type of information but generally, for a number of reasons, this has been found to be unsatisfactory. In particular, it is difficult to relate the incentive to the information supplied.

For example, should it relate to the number of pieces of information, its value to the company or the difficulty of obtaining it? This problem can give rise to dissatisfaction and feelings of unfair treatment.

Other methods of obtaining customer intelligence include:

(a) attending open house or trade shows;
(b) reading annual reports and attending annual shareholders' meetings;
(c) talking to ex-employees of customers who have moved to other companies;
(d) reading the trade press, newspapers and similar publications.

Developing information systems

The collection of a large number of separate pieces of information is of little use unless it is possible to bring the information together, analyse it and make sure that it is brought to the attention of the personnel who can make the necessary decisions and act upon it. What sort of mechanisms are required? The team meeting mentioned in the preceding chapter provides a good mechanism for exchanging information and keeping all concerned updated on the changes within customers. The effectiveness of these meetings in this respect will depend on how well they are structured and how often they are held. Unfortunately, it is usually the case that such meetings will either be held infrequently or not at all.

In developing the appropriate systems, it is first necessary to decide what information is required, and how it will be obtained. The form reproduced in Figure 6.2 shows how a capital goods supplier obtained information about his competitors. This form was issued to all staff who had contact with the customer and was returned to the desk sales engineer who decided its circulation and obtained the necessary copies.

The responsibility for obtaining information about changes within the major customer such as new staff, forthcoming enquiries, expansion plans, new sites and reorganisations was that of the outside sales engineer. The appropriate form is reproduced in Figure 6.3 and it will be noted that it is headed 'Action request form'. This meant that the form was only completed when specific action was required from others in the company. Such action might include updating the master record, calculating and supplying a budget price, sending a maintenance engineer and expediting delivery. The emphasis on 'action' had the effect of ensuring that only essential, and some desirable, information was sent back, an important requirement, since the sales engineer traditionally sent in very extensive visit reports covering almost everything that occurred during the visit, 'just in case' it was needed at some time. Unfortunately, there was so much information that management had difficulty in deciding what was important, what required action and what was merely of general interest. The action request form which replaced the regular visit report concentrated the attention of the outside sales engineers on the essential items. The inside desk sales engineer decided the circulation.

For a fast moving customer goods company the 'Promotion advice form' is simply a special application of the Action request form. A typical example is shown in Figure 6.4, demonstrating the variety of uses for this type of form.

To bring all the relevant information together, it is useful to create a *master customer book* or *fact file*. This document is generally divided into a number of sections including:

(a) customer details: names, addresses, category of business;
(b) contact names, positions, locations, comments;
(c) future customer plans;
(d) terms of business;

Source of information obtained	M. Sharpe	Area 5

Source of
information obtained ..M..Sharpe............................ **Area** ..5..................................

.....Buyer................................

.....L K Cutlery Ltd.................. **Date** ..July..1978.....................

.....Sheffield...........................

....

.... **Products** ..Hydraulic..Presses........

....

Competitor(s) 1 ..Company A.... | For circulation to

2 ..Company B....

....

Details	Office comments
Competitor A Price 10% below ours. Delivery 6 months. Installation engineer to be on site for 3 months. Rumoured to be having cash flow problems. Asking for staged payment.	**Competitor B** Price 5% higher than ours. Delivery 9 months. New sales engineer calling on this customer.	

Compiled by ....

Figure 6.2   Competitive information form

Company .... Date	For circulation	Action by
Address .... Tel. No.		
.... Outside Sales...........		
.... Engineer.................		
....		

Write to or contact

Name	Position	Address (if different from above)

Summarise actions required.   Where relevant include project/quotation/order
reference and attach detailed visit report,
questionnaires, etc., as necessary

	Action by	Final date

Compiled by ....

Figure 6.3   Action request form

Date:

Promotion
No.

Sales 1.
Accounts 1.
Despatch 1.
Planning 1.
Retained 1.

Advice submitted by ....

Account no. ....

Customer's full name and address	Promotion cost	Additional balance

Buying in period	Selling out period	Prom. discount rate	Advertising allowance
From _____	From _____ To _____		

	Code no.	Full name/s of line/s promoted	Proposed selling price	Estimated sales	Actual sales (completed by head office)		
					Week ending	No. of cases	Discount allowance
1							
2							
3							
4							

Special instructions, etc.

Area representatives concerned to be advised by head office
Yes/no

Total

Official use only

Figure 6.4   Promotion advice form

(e) buying history;

(f) share of business currently held;

(g) level of service/visits received;

(h) special activity carried out with customer (e.g. promotions, loan machines);

(i) competitive activity;

(k) annual report, press clipping, research information;

(l) quarterly customer profitability analysis;

(m) customer strategy and plans;

(n) progress against budget;

(o) action request summary.

Each company will need to build up its own headings for its fact files and it is clearly only necessary to keep these for major customers. However, once such a document has been originated for each major customer it will prove to be of inestimable value in the following areas.

1 Planning the approach to major customers.
2 Identifying trends and patterns.
3 Enabling management to make decisions to reallocate sales and service effort and highlight priorities.
4 Providing a complete picture in one place of a major source of the company's revenue and profit.

The customer fact file should be kept in the office but the salesman holding prime responsibility for the customer will often keep a condensed version for his own use. The responsibility for updating the master file will vary but could be that of the sales manager's secretary, the sales office clerk, desk sales engineer, or the marketing services assistant. The choice of who should do the updating will depend on the availability of staff, their skills and knowledge and their level of commitment to the customers concerned.

6.3 CONDUCTING CUSTOMER RESEARCH

In addition to customer intelligence the sales manager often needs specific studies of problem or opportunity areas within his major accounts. These studies may be fairly wide ranging or very specific in the information they are seeking to obtain and, for completion, will generally require the services of an outside market research or consultancy company.

The initial reaction of the sales manager to the use of an outside resource is generally one of hurt pride since he believes that he and his salesman know more about the customer than anyone else. This is very likely to be true, but there are some questions to which the salesman will find it very difficult to get correct answers.

The types of information which are often very useful for a supplier to obtain about his major customers are outlined below.

Buying process
1 How is the buying decision made?
2 Who makes the buying decision, who influences it and who initiates it?
3 What factors are taken into account in reaching a decision?
4 What buying systems are used?

Competitive activity and profiles
1 What are competitors offering?

2 What factors are considered by the buyer to be important in his choice of a supplier for a particular product or service?

3 What degree of importance or weight does the buyer attach to each of these factors?

4 How do individual suppliers rate against these factors?

5 What attributes of each competitive supplier are perceived by the buyer to be good, average or poor?

6 How do the profiles of each competitor compare and hence where do the opportunities lie for gaining a competitive advantage?

Share of business

In some cases, particularly when a supplier is selling through a distributive channel, he may not know the rate at which his products are re-selling or what the competition is selling. To find out the necessary information a sample of outlets will need to be regularly audited to ascertain their purchases, opening and closing stock by relevant product groups and brand. The A.C. Nielsen Company and Stats M.R. offer such a service to companies selling through particular types of retail outlets. Some suppliers carry out this exercise themselves on a small sample of distributive outlets.

The methods used to obtain the above information include actually purchasing the competitive products and testing them, setting up specific tests, and briefing a research agency. It is important to consult the salesman before customers are visited by other people, for three main reasons.

1 It can save considerable time in getting contact names and procedures and make certain that the questions being asked are meaningful.

2 It respects the sensitivities of the salesman and will increase his motivation to implement the results.

3 If he is not consulted, he may hear about it first from the customer itself, an incident which may lead to an unnecessary fear and suspicion of the purpose of the research.

6.4 SUMMARY

In this chapter suitable methods of collecting, storing and communicating customer information have been examined. Without such information any systematic attempt to increase the returns obtained from major customers will be a hit or miss activity.

Buyers and other personnel are often quite willing to disclose very useful information if the supplier's representatives ask questions in the right way and show that they know what to do with the answers. Thus, the buyer may not respond to the question: 'What price is competitor X quoting?' but would be much more impressed by:

Salesman: 'How does our price compare with competitor X?'

Buyer: 'Yours is a bit higher.'

Salesman: 'Ours includes a 24 hour maintenance service, free during the first year. Does theirs?'

The ability and desire of staff to carry out this function depends on their degree of commitment to this task, the organisation structure, the training they receive and the systems which exist. The salesman will generally receive training but often the service engineers, drivers and similar employees are forgotten about in this respect. Above all management must continue to motivate staff and show that they use the information obtained.

In many cases it will be necessary to supplement the customer intelligence system by more formal customer research. Many companies are loathe to spend money in this area since they feel they already know their main customers well enough. Nevertheless, much valuable information can be obtained. In particular, knowledge of how the buyers perceive the supplier compared with his competitors can help the supplier to redirect his activities in a more cost effective manner.

OBTAINING CUSTOMER INFORMATION
Action planning checklist

Questions	Answers and action	Timing of action and evaluation
1 What customer information is (a) essential (b) desirable (c) of interest		
2 What systems currently supply essential information and how can they be improved?		
3 How motivated are staff to supply the essential information? Is further training required?		
4 Has a major customer 'fact file' been established? What mechanisms exist for keeping it updated?		
5 What customer information can only be obtained by market research?		

7
Conducting the relationship

7.1 INTRODUCTION

Earlier chapters have looked at many aspects of the handling of major customers, from determining overall company policy to developing the most suitable organisation structure and to detailed customer planning. This chapter discusses the end product of all this careful preparation – the development of positive relationships with major customers and obtaining profitable business.

With existing customers, established relationships will have grown up over a period of years, often as a result of the activities of one salesman. When this salesman retires or leaves, or when a new account is being opened, the supplier has an opportunity to formulate a new relationship with the customer to make sure that profitable sales are maintained. If he does so effectively he will maintain the advantage; if he fails to, he will probably be at a continuing disadvantage.

The onus for developing the right relationship is that of the executive who holds prime responsibility for the customer. During the early stages of developing an account this is likely to be the pioneering salesman who is often working at a relatively low level within the customer. As the relationship matures, responsibility may move higher in the supplier's organisation and a distinction may be made between high level customer responsibility and day-to-day customer handling. The former may involve the commercial director in agreeing annual contract prices and maintaining high level customer relationships. The latter will be concerned with obtaining regular orders and solving delivery problems, for example.

Often these relationships develop in a fortuitous way. The salesman becomes a manager who then becomes a director. Likewise the assistant buyer is promoted to a senior position within his organisation. The contacts, therefore, that started at a low level may, over the years, move upwards. There is no doubt that such developments are desirable, but they are too important to be left to mere chance. With major customers knowing the 'right' people is as important as having the 'right' products.

7.2 TYPES OF CUSTOMER/SUPPLIER RELATIONSHIPS

It is necessary to distinguish three types of relationships:

- (a) formal customer/supplier relationships;
- (b) informal customer/supplier relationships;
- (c) informal customer/customer relationships.

Formal customer/supplier relationships

This category covers all the business interactions between buyer and seller such as (a) buyer to salesman, (b) managing director to marketing director, (c) goods inwards manager to delivery driver, (d) accounts manager to credit clerk, (e) E.D.P. manager to programmers, (f) section foreman to service engineer. The interaction between the individuals concerned is on a formal level. Generally there is some specific business matter to be taken care of such as (a) price discussions, (b) quality problems, (c) delivery schedule, (d) future requirement. Both parties recognise that each has a job to do as part of his role within his organisation. Each will perform his function to achieve his job objectives.

Without the mutual business interest it is unlikely that either party would ever meet and certainly would never develop a relationship. It is formal interaction that provides the basis. This means that unless all is functioning well formally, little can effectively be done informally. If, for example, the salesman just cannot get on the same wavelength as the buyer, there is no point in the marketing director having a quiet word in the ear of the purchasing director.

The importance of a supplier getting his formal relationships right is fundamental. He must decide who is to talk to whom to maximise the overall effect. In many cases the supplier will get it wrong. For example, a salesman having been trained to find the decision-maker in the customer's organisation may find himself face-to-face with the managing director without the ability or skill to handle the situation. Conversely, after opening up major new customers the marketing director may remove himself totally from maintaining business with the customer, much to the annoyance of the customer's senior management who feel they have been 'demoted' in their supplier's eyes.

Informal customer/supplier relationships

'All the best deals are struck on the golf course.' Besides the formal relationship, informal buyer/seller relationships are possible and even desirable. They help lubricate the business process and enhance the fruitfulness of the formal relationship. As well as joint sporting activities other elements include (a) lunches and dinners, (b) theatre visits, (c) cocktail parties, (d) visits to a sporting occasion.

Supplier/customer informal relationships are useful in helping the formal process. They can only occur if the formal relationships are basically sound. It is perfectly possible to conduct business with major customers successfully without developing any informal relationship. However, if they are developed, it makes the total interaction less difficult and further cements the supplier/customer relationship. It is, therefore, necessary to think about the informal as well as the formal interaction. The relationship must not be abused, nor should it be used in a cold or calculated manner but, at least in outline, it should enter into the planning procedure for major customers.

The onus is on the supplier to develop a network of contacts with his customer. A number of individuals on the supplier's side at varying levels and in a variety of functions must interact with a larger number of customer personnel. Only in this manner can the supplier make certain that he is not solely dependent on one employee or one customer contact for the business. When either of these individuals changes position or leaves, the business with the customer is at risk. Not only does a multiplicity of contacts safeguard the supplier, it also facilitates expansion of sales to the customer should this be desirable.

Informal customer/customer relationships

Buyers, engineers, marketing personnel and all others in the customer's organisation will be members of informal groups, as well as fulfilling their formal role within the company. These informal groups include:

    (a)   other buyers, engineers, marketing staff from inside and outside the company;
    (b)   senior company executives;
    (c)   government bodies, banks, other financing sources;
    (d)   customers, local press.

A buying decision for an industrial service may be subject to the buyer checking first with another buyer from a different company already using the supplier. At a professional society dinner, an engineer may discuss a particular piece of equipment with another member who is also considering its purchase. In making a decision to repackage his products, the marketing director will wish to take into account what his customers think about it.

These types of interaction can be of vital importance. Sometimes a supplier will lose an order not knowing why. The normal excuses of price and delivery may not seem appropriate. All formal and informal relationships appear to be operating well. In this case it may very well be that a buyer in another company or maybe the customer's bank has expressed reservations about the deal.

The supplier can only control this process to a limited extent. Clearly his formal and informal contacts must be spread to cover as many influencers as is feasible but it is rarely possible to contact or even know all of them. His best defence is to make sure his products live up to expectation and his overall customer service meets the market needs. In addition the following may be implemented.

    1   If a major customer is displeased, time should be spent on reducing his displeasure.
    2   Customers should be supplied with reference lists of successful applications and contented customers to supplement their formal and informal channels.
    3   The supplier should ensure that the sales effort is appropriate to the type of customer. One buyer commenting about the high pressure selling techniques of a certain supplier said 'Their salesmen are so busy trying to get an order, they never bother to find out what I need!'

7.3 OBTAINING, DEVELOPING AND MAINTAINING BUSINESS

The planning process described in Chapter 5 details *what* needs to be done to achieve the objectives set for individual major customers. Section 7.2 described the interpersonal relationship network within which this must take place. We now look at how the relationship develops over time and the sales techniques which must be used. It is important to distinguish between the various stages of the relationship between buyer and seller. The development of this relationship is depicted in Figure 7.1.

Obtaining the initial order

Initially, when the supplier is seeking to obtain his first order from a major customer he will, as shown in Figure 7.1, be predominantly selling to him. In effect, the supplier has to persuade the buyer that he has a need for his offering, that the offering satisfies that need and that the price is right. This is the sales approach around which most sales presentations and sales training are structured. Traditionally the salesman has been instructed to follow a number of steps.

1 Plan the sales interview.
2 Open the interview by asking questions about customer needs.
3 Make presentation of offering and its benefits to meet customer needs.
4 Handle and overcome objections raised by customer.
5 Close the sale and get customer to buy.

He has been told that this works because the buyer's mind goes through five successive mental states known as AIDAS:

1. Attention
2. Interest
3. Desire
4. Action
5. Satisfaction

That this approach and theory have limitations does not reduce their successful use in obtaining business initially with a large customer. Generally, these initial orders will be

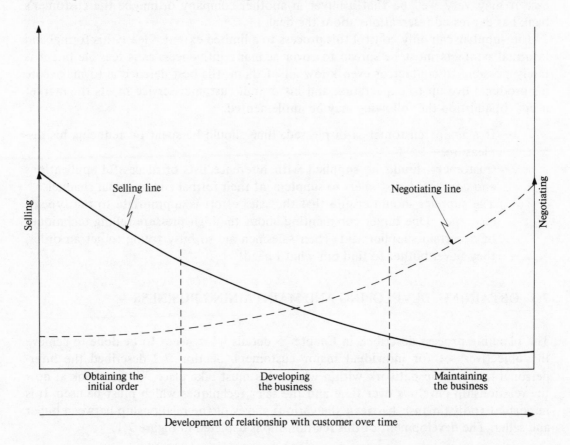

Figure 7.1   Development of buyer/seller relationship

relatively small. A multiple supermarket buyer may decide to test a few products from the supplier's total range in a few, selected stores. The machine shop manager in a factory may wish to test a new supplier's cutting oil on a couple of lathes. The buyer needs to be convinced that the product will satisfy his needs better than that which he currently buys. This is a typical 'new purchase situation' described in Chapter 1.

To obtain new customers is one of the most difficult jobs that the traditional salesman has to do, since it will tend to be more complex and occur over a longer time period than obtaining orders from established customers. Where these prospects are very large, the perceived task may be so enormous that the salesman may 'abort' almost as soon as he has started. However, by carefully planning his approach, and limiting his initial objectives, the overall complexity can be reduced. Thus, for example, the initial objective with a new prospect may be to obtain a small 'trial' order, restricting contact to the assistant buyer and shop floor personnel. Alternatively, it may just be to obtain information about the customer's organisation structure and current sources of supply.

Developing the business

After the supplier has obtained his initial foothold with the customer, he must reinforce and expand it. The prime purpose is to consolidate the success achieved, make it an established and recognised fact and set the scene for future action.

The amount of selling that takes place is reduced as compared to the initial phase of obtaining the order as shown in Figure 7.1. The amount of negotiation, however, increases. This is because both parties begin to accept that the product or service does satisfy the buyer's need. A selling job still needs to be done to build orders but increasingly other factors such as price, delivery, support, credit and discounts will become important.

At this stage the supplier must seek to expand his contacts and begin to develop the formal and informal customer relationships discussed in section 7.2. Whether this is the responsibility of the salesman or a group will depend upon individual circumstances, but it is vitally important for whoever is responsible to be aware that the development of the right relationships is a key factor at this stage if the supplier is to move successfully to the next stage. Thus, the manager needs not only to ask himself 'how much business are we getting from Customer X?' but also 'who do we know in Customer X, who else do we need to know and what sort of relationship do we have?'

Maintaining the business

Once entrenched as the established supplier the amount of selling required is substantially reduced. In effect the task is one of (a) effective servicing, (b) negotiation, (c) control. The buyer faces a typical 'repeat purchase' situation.

Effective servicing covers all the activities associated with ensuring that the customer remains happy with the supplier and his offering. To assist in this effort the supplier should implement a control system as discussed in Chapter 9.

The increasing importance of negotiation, as opposed to selling (Figure 7.1), comes about because the relationship between buyer and seller has reached the following stages.

1 The buyer will continue to buy, unless he is prevented from doing so by outside forces.
2 The customer's organisation is attuned to the supplier's product or service, e.g. everyone is used to seeing green boxes in the stock room or Fred on the production floor.
3 The supplier is well integrated with the customer.

Thus, the buyer does not talk about whether he will or will not buy the supplier's product, but of the terms and conditions at which the transaction is made. The traditional salesman who is not aware of this situation will tend to give away a large number of concessions to a professional buyer to secure an order he can already rely on getting.

By developing a larger number of informal relationships the supplier can ensure that the customer continues to be serviced effectively. Often this will involve senior management, as well as salesmen, interacting with the buyer. In many instances companies can attribute the loss of a major customer to the fact that such informal relationships have not developed sufficiently during this stage.

Capital goods selling

The process described of obtaining, developing and maintaining the customer's business is not strictly applicable to capital goods selling. In this case customers will order infrequently, order size will be large and lead times long. The result is that although the three phases which characterise the development of the relationship with the customer are still valid, they are now associated with each separate order as shown in Figure 7.2. This illustrates the various steps involved in obtaining a high value capital goods order. Steps 1 to 7 can be regarded as the initial stage of obtaining agreement, steps 8 and 9 developing the business and step 10 onwards maintaining the business.

It should be noted that in many highly complex projects steps 3, 4 and 5 may all be repeated more than once, before step 6 is arrived at, and even this stage can be repeated on some occasions.

The continuing operation of the informal supplier/customer relationships is important and can often give early warning of potentially adverse occurrences. This will allow rectifying action to be taken.

7.4 SUMMARY

This chapter has examined the nature of the relationship between the supplier and his major customers and how this develops over time. In particular, it has been stressed that the informal relationship becomes more useful after the supplier has opened up the account and is developing and maintaining the business. In turn this has implications for the information and control systems discussed in the previous chapter. The manager must be concerned not only with the amount of business being carried out with the customer but also with how his salesmen are developing their relationships. Mechanisms for monitoring this are the Action request form and Major customer information format.

The development of the informal relationship is vital between all levels of staff if the major customer is to be retained on a secure basis. Failure to develop this relationship effectively with customer staff can result in a loss of that customer when individual personalities move or leave. Also it allows competition to attack from a variety of directions. Often the supplier becomes aware of such an attack only when the competition is too well entrenched and the battle is all but over.

As the relationship with the customer develops the necessity will increase for the salesman to negotiate, as opposed to sell. This clearly has implications for the knowledge and skill that the salesman must have and the training he should be given. This will be discussed in Chapter 8.

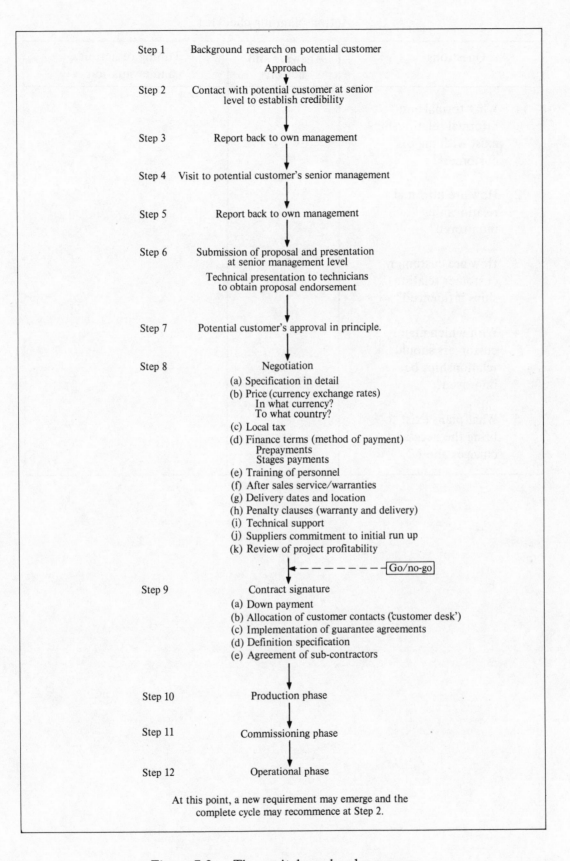

Figure 7.2   The capital goods sales process

Action planning checklist

Questions	Answers and action	Timing of action and evaluation
1 What formal and informal relationships exist with major customers?		
2 How are informal relationships monitored?		
3 How are customer/ customer relation- ships influenced?		
4 With which major customers should relationships be improved?		
5 What plans exist to bring the necessary changes about?		

8
Implementing the customer plan

8.1 INTRODUCTION

To implement the major customer plans effectively both management and staff must upgrade their knowledge and skills. This will involve training which must cover sales staff and sales support staff who have significant customer contact. This chapter discusses the three main aspects of the implementation – negotiation, visits by sales support staff to customers and the conducting of factory visits by customers. Experience shows that these are the main areas where individual skills need to be developed. It is intended as a guide to the senior sales and marketing manager in helping him review the current training to assess how well it covers the important aspects of each subject area.

8.2 NEGOTIATION

Once the relationship between buyer and seller has developed to a point where the need to buy is largely in balance with the need to supply, then negotiation can take place. It is taken as self-evident, therefore, in a negotiation situation that in the final analysis the buyer needs the supplier's products because he makes his profits in meeting his customers' needs, and the supplier's products enable him to do so. This is rarely discussed or even admitted during negotiations, but it provides the bedrock for such discussions.

As examined in Chapter 7 successful sales techniques produce the basis for any negotiation when the customer, having made the fundamental buying decision, then focuses on the many detailed factors surrounding the decision. The emphasis moves towards the profit implications of the decision and how the supplier can increase the customer's sales or reduce his costs or liberate his time to get on with other matters. Many factors enter into these considerations. They include price, discounts, bonuses, allowances, product specification, product packaging, staff training, delivery frequency and location.

In the process of seeking to obtain agreement on all these 'terms and conditions' *compromise* is inevitable. It is this factor of compromise which provides the basic matter of negotiations. This element of controlled compromise, which must be recognised to ensure profit to both sides, often clashes with the inflexible nature of many sales techniques. Generally, the more 'hard sell' the sales approach, the more difficult the transition. It is of interest to note, for example, that in the office equipment industry, where hard selling has traditionally been the order of the day, relatively few companies have systematically tackled large customers successfully and most make a financial loss out of such transactions. It is those companies which have softened their approach that tend to be more successful.

Having recognised the nature of the negotiation situation, the salesman must leave the security of his fixed position and bring about final agreement by moving, or appearing to move, towards the customer and inducing reciprocal movement from the customer. Recognition of this fact is the critical step, after which time the supplier's salesman can make sure that each move costs as little as possible, and elicits as great a movement as possible on the buyer's behalf.

In Table 8.1 the negotiation principles checklist is reproduced from John Lidstone's book, *Negotiating Profitable Sales*. It is vital that the negotiator bears these principles in mind. The reader may care to recall the last negotiation with which he was involved and assess his own performance against the principles listed.

Table 8.1   Negotiation principles checklist

	Principle	Comments
1	Negotiation is the act or process of bargaining to reach a mutually acceptable agreement or objective.	Both sides must feel they have won, but not regret what the other side has achieved because it is not seen as gained at his expense. Each side achieves what it feels is most important.
2	Negotiation must take place between equals – in each other's eyes.	Although titles may be different, the ability of either side to make matching decisions is essential as is the mutual respect between negotiators that both count as equals.
3	Negotiation is based on a common respect for the rules of the game.	Be yourself. Discuss rather than debate. Neither side must attempt 'one-up-manship'. At the same time neither side yields anything that is really important to him, although he may well indicate the opposite. Avoid domination.
4	Put your cards on the table.	Do not pretend negotiating powers you do not possess. Declare what you can do and what you cannot do.
5	Be patient.	In negotiation, rushed decisions are rarely good ones that satisfy either side. Be prepared to take time and don't hurry. Delay is better than a bad decision.
6	See the other side's case, unemotionally.	Often called empathy, being able to put yourself in the negotiating position of the person opposite you, without being blinkered or emotionally involved, helps your assessment of his position.
7	Communicate to advance relationship and negotiation objectives.	Be open and disclose your motives and self-interest. Lay it on the line and let the buyer do so in turn. Don't be obscure.

Table 8.1   (continued)

	Principle	Comments
8	Avoid confrontation.	Don't put yourself in a position from which you cannot retract. If you have a row things are said which can make negotiating impossible. Avoid showdowns. Stand firm but always state your position calmly.
9	If you disagree do so as from a devil's advocate position.	Be prepared to disagree by looking at your case from the buyer's point of view. This enables you to say things that do not confront the buyer nor give rise to a confrontation.
10	Give a bit at a time.	Never concede everything or nothing. Give slice by slice, but for every concession you give get one back: 'If you do this I will do that'.
11	Know when to leave well alone.	In negotiation there is rarely an ideal solution, so don't pursue one when it is beyond your reach, too costly or takes more time than you can afford.
12	Declare company strategies if you must, but not objectives behind them.	Company strategies and plans become public knowledge as soon as they are implemented, but the objectives, personal motivations and needs that give them birth, impetus and fuel them should be kept secret.
13	Don't compromise your ultimate objectives.	Set your highest and lowest negotiating objective, then don't settle below the lowest point. Lose rather than gain a worthless deal.
14	Never relax your guard.	Stamina is one of the hallmarks of a good negotiator. Your opponent may stall for hours just to find out when you will crack. If you can't bide your time in such duels don't negotiate.
15	Always rehearse your case.	Tell yourself what you are going to say, how you are going to say it and when. Then rehearse how your opposite numbers will do the same.
16	Do not underestimate other people.	Many negotiators pretend not to know or to be foolish. Some are fools, but others may appear so to mislead you.

Table 8.1 (continued)

	Principle	Comments
17	Respect confidences given in negotiating.	Don't ever betray a confidence learnt during negotiation. The essence of negotiation is mutual trust.
18	End negotiations positively.	Satisfactory negotiations should end when both sides can part without regret. Try to end all negotiations on a positive basis of satisfying the needs of all parties.

Planning the negotiation

In any negotiation the seller and the buyer both wish to achieve their objectives. Both know they must reach a point of balance by a series of compromises which form the ingredients of the negotiation. This process is represented diagrammatically in Figure 8.1. Therefore, the planning process needs to take account of each of the four key

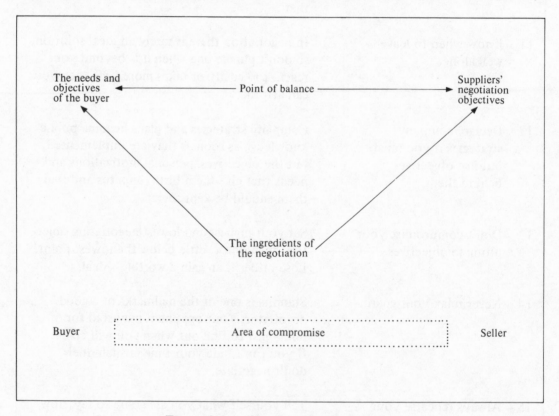

Figure 8.1 The negotiation process

elements of the negotiation and the interaction between them. This is accomplished by the supplier approaching the planning in six steps.
1 Assess the objective and subjective buyer needs.
2 From these, isolate the key areas for negotiation.
3 Compare the costs and value (both real and perceived).

4 Assess both the likely actual stances to be adopted by the buyer and the likely stated stances with which he will open the negotiation.

5 Relate these to the commercial and marketing objectives set by the supplier.

6 Decide the actual and opening stances to be adopted relative to the buyer's and plan the conduct of the interview.

To facilitate the planning process a checklist, Table 8.2, examines each of the six steps in greater detail. Consideration of these points before a negotiation will greatly increase the chance of a successful outcome.

Table 8.2 Checklist for negotiation planning

---

1 *Assessing the needs*
 (a) What are the customer's marketing policies?
 (b) What are his major marketing strategies?
 (c) What are his markets?
   For example:
   Which market segment does he concentrate on?
   If a distributor, what share of his business does he expect to be derived from our products?
   How is he organised relative to his markets?
 (d) What marketing tactics does he use?
   For example:
   Is he keen on promotions?
   Does he pass on promotional discounts to *his* customers?
   How many salesmen does he have?
   What is the level of professionalism of his salesmen?'
   Do they need training?
   Is he advertising-oriented?
   Does he approve of merchandising material?
   Does he like incentives for himself or his staff?
 (e) What space or time does he really have available for our products?
 (f) Which competitors does he favour or have a grudge against?
 (g) What are the commercial needs of the buyer?
 (h) In what ways does the purchase or non-purchase of our products affect his business or processes?
 (i) What problems does he have? (Look at production/sales/personnel/finance.)
 (j) What alternatives are open to him?
 (k) What are his subjective needs?
 (l) How important are they?

2 *Main areas or ingredients of negotiation*
 (a) What is important to the buyer in making his decision?
 (b) What areas will he seek to negotiate most keenly?
 (c) What combination of factors will he want? For example:
   Cost – Price – Volume – Promotional support – Delivery terms – Credit – Availability – Training – Brand Name – Exclusive Terms – Specification – After sales service, etc.

Table 8.2   (continued)

3 *Costs and value of concessions in these areas*
   (a)   What concessions does the buyer offer?
   (b)   What will he expect to exchange?
   (c)   What will be the cost to both sides relative to the returns in each area?
   (d)   Which concessions, of little cost to us, will be of considerable value to the buyer?
   (e)   Which concessions are most expensive?
   (f)   Within what range are we each likely to operate?

4 *Assess the buyer's stances*
   (a)   What is the real strength of the buyer's need?
   (b)   How will he *state* the strength of his need by his opening stance?
   (c)   What means will he use to pull us towards this position?
   (d)   What is our estimate of the actual stance the buyer will take after negotiation?

5 *Relate these to our own objectives*
   (a)   What do we need to achieve?
   (b)   In what ways do the buyer's stances match or conflict with our objectives?
   (c)   Can any major differences be resolved by negotiation?

6 *Decide our stances and plan the conduct of negotiation*
   (a)   What bargaining points do we have?
   (b)   How can the value of these to the buyer be raised relative to the cost to us?
   (c)   What concessions can be expected from the buyer and how do these match our bargaining points?
   (d)   Where should the negotiation take place?
   (e)   Who should be involved?
   (f)   Should particular points be dealt with individually or does the buyer need a 'package'?
   (g)   How can the interview be planned to give us opportunity to seek agreement at each stage?

An example will be useful to illustrate the main points. Consider the case of steel salesmen selling to an engineering company buyer.

   1   Objective and subjective buyer needs
   (a) Objective – Price, discount.
                    Delivery – promptness and frequency.
                    Back-up stocks held by supplier.
                    Quality (taken for granted).
                    Credit facilities.
   (b) Subjective – Must appear to be buying well.
                    Must keep production manager happy.
                    Prefers to buy British.
                    Desires long term relationship with supplier.

2   *Main areas for negotiation*
   (a)   What is included in the price?
   (b)   Delivery schedule and penalties for failure to maintain schedule on both sides.
   (c)   Right of redress in case of quality problems.
   (d)   Settlement time.
   (e)   Price increases.
   (f)   Handling of orders outside agreed schedule.
   Clearly buyer and seller will have different views in each area, e.g. buyer will want fixed prices, seller will want to pass on all price increases.

3   *Cost and value of concessions in each area*
   (a)   Price
         Estimated 10% price increase over contract period.
         Total contract value £80,000.
         Therefore, cost of fixed price £8,000.
   (b)   Delivery
         Delivery schedule will be kept to, provided supplier has product in stock, which is very likely during contract period.
         Value to customer of assured supply is:
         reduction in stock levels by £10,000: at 12% interest p.a. this is worth £100 per month;
         assurance of continuity of production, which may be worth up to £20,000 per day plus 'peace of mind'.
   Similarly, the other negotiation areas can be costed both quantitatively and qualitatively.

4   *Actual and stated stances by buyer*
   (a)   Actual
         Maximum discount.
         Fixed delivery schedule.
         Right to source elsewhere besides contract supplier.
         All poor quality product replaced in two days.
   Note: In present surplus supply conditions he will use threat of going to smaller competitor.
   (b)   Stated
         Maximum discount.
         Fixed prices.
         Fixed delivery schedule and penalty for failure to adhere by supplier.
         Sixty days' credit.
   Note: He must buy steel and he is used to dealing with this supplier.

5   *Relate stances to supplier's own objectives*
   Objectives:
   To increase volume sales at acceptable margins by $y\%$.
   To obtain more contract orders to provide base load business.
   To increase return on investment by $x\%$.
   Note: Supplier can afford to give maximum discount as this maintains the minimum gross margin. Fixed prices are unacceptable since this will reduce margins below minimum. They will only be acceptable if customer pays on receipt of goods.

6   *Supplier's actual and stated opening stances*
    (a)   Actual
        Maximum discount.
        Fixed delivery schedule.
        Variable price to reflect cost increases.
        Sole supplier of all steel.
        Quality problems replaced in 1 week.
        Credit 30 days.
        Willing to hold back-up stocks.
    (b)   Stated
        Less than maximum discount.
        Delivery schedule variable by ± 5 days.
        Variable price.
        Quality problems replaced in 10 days.
        Not willing to hold specific back-up stocks.

There are a number of important concessions the supplier could offer which cost relatively little:
        Fixed delivery schedule.
        Quality problem replacement.
        Specific back-up stocks.

In addition, he is a major UK supplier and thus the concessions on back-up stock and so on are more likely to be credible. Further, having negotiated such a good deal with the reputable supplier the buyer will be seen to be doing a good job.

Conducting the negotiation

The art of negotiation involves the trading of concessions. Where these cost the supplier little but are perceived as very valuable by the customer, and thereby elicit valuable reciprocal concessions, then the supplier is skilled in the art.

Usually the buyer will overstate his initial stance: 'There's no point in talking to me about a new management information system, I've got figures coming out of my ears', or, 'All right let's talk about it, but I warn you, the deal will have to be good for me even to consider it.'

It is useful to look at what *to do* and what *not to do* during a negotiation.

Do

1   Keep objectives clearly in mind.
2   Determine who has what authority early on. Where it is a one to one negotiation, e.g. salesman/buyer, then make sure buyer has authority to yield required concessions. Where it is a team negotiation find out how individuals relate to each other and who makes the decision.
3   In foreign or unusual situations forward information must be obtained, e.g. the language in which negotiations will be conducted, a description of local conditions.
4   Maintain self-control and the initiative without being hostile.
5   Allow buyer to do most of the talking in the early stages.
6   Move discussion from opening stances to a clear statement of actual stances.
7   Trade concessions one at a time.
8   Increase value of concessions given to buyer.

9   Devalue concessions given by buyer.

10   Have facts and figures at hand.

11   Recap often and summarise before ending interview.

12   Get agreement in principle when firm settlements are not possible; it leaves the door open to resume negotiations at a later date.

13   Be aware of face and body movements which may be more reflective of true feelings than the words used, e.g. arms crossed may mean suspicion, tightly clenched fists may mean frustration, doodling may mean boredom.

Don't

1   Do not reveal your position too quickly.

2   Do not make a concession unless something is obtained in return.

3   Do not frustrate the buyer by not answering his direct questions.

4   Do not drive too hard a bargain or dig your heels in.

5   Do not allow the buyer to lose face.

6   Do not take a stance prematurely which may result in negotiations reaching a point of no return.

7   Do not talk down to the buyer.

8   Do not be 'pat' or 'glib'.

9   Do not belabour issues on which agreement is difficult to reach.

10   Do not ask emotional questions, e.g. 'Why do you feel that way?'

11   Do not present the buyer with unacceptable alternatives.

For team negotiation:

12   Do not argue with colleague team members.

13   Do not overplay the 'good guy'/'bad guy' roles.

14   Do not allow fragmented conversations across the main stream.

Team negotiations

Many sales negotiations particularly for large value business will involve at least two representatives from the buyer and seller's side. The same principles and dos and don'ts apply but a further dimension is added because of the numbers of people involved.

It is necessary for the supplier to establish clearly the roles of each individual on his team to avoid the last three 'do nots' listed above. Also it must be established who will speak and who will not. Otherwise the tendency is for the individual who has not spoken to do so at a most inopportune time in a most inopportune way.

Four roles must be covered by the supplier during the negotiation.

1   Spokesman: presents the case, responds to the other side, initiates tactics, makes decisions, implements strategy, maintains the initiative. Generally this will be the senior man – the team captain.

2   Specialist support: enters into the negotiation at the specific request of the spokesman, either pre-arranged or during the meeting. He presents detailed aspects relevant to his own specialism. Generally, this will be the salesman, engineer, contracts manager, designer, etc.

3   Recorder: keeps a step-by-step account of how events are developing, as impartially as possible. He should be sitting close to the spokesman as this will help the latter during his periodic summaries.

4   Analysts: to provide detailed analytical support.

It is important that the spokesman has the ability to manage the team and allocate tasks, has personal responsibility for, and identifies with, the result, has the authority to make the necessary decisions and the intellectual capacity to handle a fast moving, complex situation. In capital goods negotiation the sales team may be facing not only the customer's personnel, but also representatives from the financing sources, sub-contractors and even government. Figure 8.2 shows the interactions involved in obtaining a capital goods order overseas.

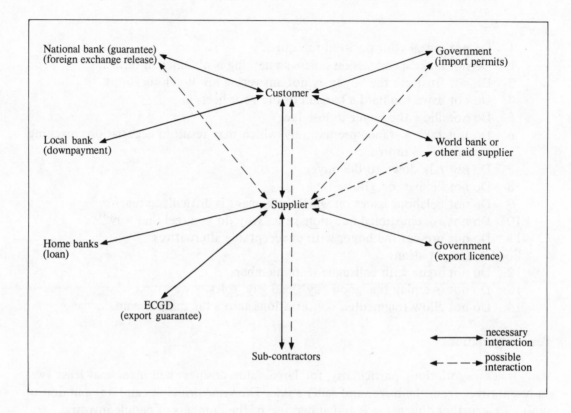

Figure 8.2   Multidimensional overseas capital goods negotiation

Because of their complexity, team negotiations can take a long time to conclude. This requires that the participants prepare carefully and that they possess considerable mental and physical stamina. It is important to maintain an alert appearance which will be helped by the calling of a number of breaks. In addition, it is useful for the spokes-man to have a deputy to whom he can hand over whilst he takes time to recover.

Generally, the venue will be the buyer location but if this can be avoided so much the better. Likewise the seating will be arranged by the customer, but if the spokesman can establish himself at the head of the table this will facilitate control of the meeting.

In preparation the team must plan for the negotiation. In particular, the following points must be considered, agreed and understood.

1   Each person's role. It is perfectly possible for an individual to adopt more than one role, or for several participants to share a role.
2   The negotiation strategy – customer and supplier.
3   Tactics to be employed – customer and supplier.
4   What must *not* happen, i.e. the don'ts.

5   How the spokesman will bring colleagues into the discussion.
6   How matters will be brought to the attention of the spokesman.
7   Points that cannot be conceded.

8.3   THE SUPPORT FUNCTION

As we have seen, the effective handling of major customers involves a number of people from the supplier's side, including the applications engineer, the finance director, the distribution manager, the credit control clerk and the contracts manager. How should they conduct their relationship with major customers? In many cases a problem is created when these individuals interact with the customer. This arises, in part, because of the very qualities they possess that make them so valuable to the supplier in their internal job. For example, the ability of the engineer to identify, analyse and solve problems is extremely merit-worthy. However, if he focuses solely on the problems in front of the customer, assuming the virtues of the product are self-evident, he may do more harm than good. The financial man whose dispassionate attitude is vital to the objective analysis and control of the business may appear aloof, condescending and 'know all' to the buyer.

The support staff therefore, have dealings with customers which can:

(a)   affect the view of the customer or prospect of the supplier and, hence, the relationship between the two companies;

(b)   when providing advice during a sale, assist or damage the progress of the sale;

(c)   result in the supplier entering into unacceptable commitments or obligations with the customer;

(d)   gain information about the prospect/customer and his needs which may be of value to the marketing/sales department;

(e)   through the advice given to a prospect, and the way it is given, virtually conclude a sale.

It is useful to look at two aspects of the specialist support man's function in this respect – making the visit to the customer, and conducting the factory visit.

Visits to customers

This may take place for a number of reasons including to assist in the sale, to resolve a customer complaint or problem, to provide technical, financial or other advice. To carry out this function effectively the staff concerned should structure their approach as follows:

1   Plan the call, i.e. prepare themselves for the visit.
2   Set call objectives.
3   Establish customer/prospect needs.
4   Present the benefits of the advice or products being discussed.
5   Conduct the interview and deal with the objections to the advice given.
6   Handling of complaints.

The checklist in Table 8.3 will be useful in assisting the relevant personnel to carry out their vital part in the relationship with major customers.

Table 8.3   Effective customer visits for non-sales personnel – checklist

1   *Planning the call*
    (a) Finding out about the customer
         Make use of the following:

Briefing notes supplied by the salesman concerned or his sales manager.
Verbal briefing given by the salesman concerned.
The data in an inspection report if there is one.

The data on the quotation or specification if there is one.
Files and customer records.
Customer's correspondence if any.
Knowledge of the customer held by colleagues including desk salesmen.
The customer master 'fact file'.

    (b) When making a call on a prospect to help the sale
         The following information should be obtained from the *salesman* concerned:

What is the history of our dealings with the company?
When was the last call made?
Who are we dealing with in the customer's company?
What the customer makes?
What the applications are?
What are the customer's needs?

Which products were presented?
What product benefits are crucial to the customer?
The information or advice the customer wants from the technical man?
The salesman's advice on how the technical man:
(1)   should play his role in the interview;
(2)   can most help the salesman to gain business.

    (c) When making a call on a customer concerning a complaint or a problem
         The following information should be found:

Who has been dealing with complaint/problem so far?
What do we know about the complaint or problem at this stage?
What is the history of our dealings with the company?
Have we experience of similar complaints or problems elsewhere, and what does it tell us?

Have we experience of complaints or problems with this customer?
What has he bought and when?
What does he make?
What are his processes/applications?
What did our quotation say?
What are the relevant terms of our agreement with the customer?

2   *Setting the call objective*
    For each call, an objective should be set.
    Is the objective clear and specific?
    Does it state what has to be achieved on the call?
    Is it formally recorded?

Table 8.3 (continued)

3 *Establish likely customer needs which your advice should meet*

These needs might include:

Need to meet specific requirements re tolerance, lengths, etc.
Appropriateness to quality-critical applications.
Best product to meet technical requirements.
Need to meet quality requirements, test certificates, etc.
Provision of test facilities.

Product reliability.
Product appearance.
Economical life/use of product.
Low replacement costs.
Need to meet his customer's contract deadlines.
Need for technical support on an ongoing basis.
Need to meet financial constraints.

4 *Present the benefits to the customer of the products you present or of the advice you give*

These might include:

Quality of product and test certificates.
Reliability of product.
Appropriateness to quality critical applications.
Ability to meet specification.
Reduction in finished component costs.
Fast replacement service.

Cheaper material.
Lighter material.
Ability to supply range of products.
Economic life/use.
Reduction in material usage.
Low machining costs.
Reduction in machining time.
Low replacement costs.
Longer tool life.

5 *Conducting the visit*

Agree main purpose of visit.
Listen to what the customer has to say.
Establish and clarify in your own words the customer's needs and technical requirements.
Listen to the customer.
Assess which matters can be resolved there and then and which cannot.
Present advice logically.
Listen to the customer.
Use visual aids to clarify points.
Stress benefits, i.e. what the product does well, to counterbalance problem discussions.
Ask if the customer agrees with the feasibility of advice given.
Keep the customer's attention and ask questions.
Listen to objections.
Repeat objections in own words and present counter-benefits.
Seek to reach agreement, if necessary by asking for it.
Close on a positive note and stress what has been accomplished.

Table 8.3   (continued)

6   *Complaint handling*
Avoid blaming the customer.
Avoid blaming your colleagues.
Avoid blaming the product.
Listen carefully to the details of complaint.
Show understanding of the customer's point of view.
Clarify what he has said to ensure you have the facts right.
If the customer appears to be at fault, be diplomatic.
If the company appears to be at fault:
(a) apologise;
(b) do not accept liability;
(c) do not, at this stage, enter into definite commitments which involve your company in substantial costs.
Present your remedy, stressing the benefits to the customer of what you propose.
Secure his agreement to the action you will take.

7   *After the call*
Make sure that you carry out the action that you have undertaken.
Ensure that the customer is informed of progress.
Explain to the salesman concerned the result of your call, the current attitude of the customer, and the nature of any commitment which your company may have to accept.

Conducting factory visits

There are often a number of people involved when a customer visits a supplier's factory, including the factory manager, laboratory staff, despatch manager, sales manager, and so on. It is surprising, therefore, how often, besides vague generalisations like 'getting to know the customer better' or 'showing them our capabilities', few personnel involved have any idea as to the real reason for the visit. It is important to: (a) establish visit objectives; (b) ensure that everyone concerned is aware of what these objectives are and can tailor their activities accordingly.

Besides the supplier's objectives the visitor will have his own stated reasons for coming. These, on closer examination, may turn out to be either minor objectives or superficial camouflage, disguising the more important reasons. Some examples of reasons, stated and real, for customer visiting are shown in Table 8.4.

Having established the objectives of the visit it is next necessary to structure the occasion so that the visitor views the supplier in the best light and will be favourably disposed towards him. In this context the visit can be split into three stages:

Stage 1:   Beginning: (a) organisation, preparation and invitation;
                       (b) welcome, agreement of timetable and objectives of visit.
Stage 2:   Middle: Tour of presentation of that part of the company of interest to the visitor.
Stage 3:   End
           (a) Handling of doubts and getting agreement;
           (b) Goodbyes and post mortem.

It is up to the organiser to see that the visit is organised and conducted within this selling framework. This is by no means an easy job when the visitor will undoubtedly be meeting people not renowned for their selling, persuasion or diplomatic skills.

Table 8.4   Examples of reasons for factory visit

Type of visitor	Supplier's reason	Visitor's stated reason	Visitor's real reason
Buyer or general manager from large customer	Find out what they will be taking next quarter	To discuss his new location's goods receiving arrangements	To decide whether to find second source
Manager from company within larger organisation	To get our foot in the door	Discuss specifications	To pursue independent buying policy for political reasons
Old faithful customer	Keep him sweet – over lunch	Talk about next order	Chance to get away from pressures of office
Former customer	Bring him back into the fold	Clear up old complaint	See if the supplier's attitudes have changed
Recently acquired customer	Get the rest of his business	To discuss the trial order	Examine our capacity capabilities
Newly promoted buyer	Convert him	See what we have to offer	Learn about the product for the first time
Customer's customer	To impress our own customer	Sort out technical problem	To examine possibility of making part in-house
Agent/ Distributor	Get him off his backside	Discuss business potential in his country	Find out what is selling easily elsewhere
Foreign delegation or trade visit	Get leads, e.g. names of their competitors	To compare the technical aspects of suppliers' product and home produced product	To fill up an afternoon in the itinerary
Director's guest	To please our director	Unknown	To meet people who could be useful

To be certain that the visitor's needs are met it is essential to bear in mind the simple rules laid down in Table 8.5, and when conducting a demonstration the principles detailed in Table 8.6 should be followed.

Table 8.5   Factory visit checklist

1   *Make it easy for the visitor*
   (a) Explain what you are going to do and why.
   (b) Simplify and leave out irrelevancies.
   (c) Relate to the listener's own experience.
   (d) Get the listener to participate.
   (e) Use visual aids diagrams.
   (f) Question and be enthusiastic.
   (g) Summarise what you have done within the total context.
   (h) Don't be a 'whiz kid'.

2   *Recognise the needs of the bodily senses*
   (a) vivid explanations of danger points/steep stairs;
   (b) protective clothing and distinctive hard hats;
   (c) refreshments and toilet;
   (d) not too long on the feet.

3   *Recognise the needs of the customer's mind*
   (a) he is important and wants to be respected – prenotify reception, the dining room, etc.;
   (b) he has a point of view and wants to give it;
   (c) he wants to know how we can help him;
   (d) he wants to settle doubts, queries, snags;
   (e) he doesn't object to your summarising and pointing the way ahead.

4   *Always structure the visit itself so the visitor knows what is happening*
   (a) explain first;
   (b) show;
   (c) summarise after.

Table 8.6   Demonstrating a product or machine: checklist

1   *Before the demonstration:*
   (a) What exactly is the demonstration trying to do, e.g. prove a point, clear up a misunderstanding, develop pride of ownership, give confidence, establish performance?
   (b) Have we adequately prepared and rehearsed?

2   *During the demonstration:*
   (a) the visitor can either listen or watch so: tell – show – tell;
   (b) handle the machine or product with respect;
   (c) involve the customer.

3   *After the demonstration:*
   (a) Talk over the product and find out his feelings;
   (b) Introduce the visitor to any literature.

Finally, it is necessary to identify responsibility for the visit. All too often the salesman will tell the maintenance manager half a day before that Mr Y from Customer X is coming and would he arrange to have him 'shown round'. This is 'passing the buck' rather than accepting responsibility. Usually it will be the salesman or sales manager who does the organising but it may be a director or production man. Some companies publish a weekly list of who is visiting the company, with the name of the person responsible. The advance publication of the names of visitors, their companies and their hosts allows other interested parties to contact the sponsor and advise, warn or simply avoid duplication of contact.

The two biggest complaints of people involved with visits are that: (a) they have not had sufficient notice; (b) they have not been sufficiently briefed. This is the duty of the person responsible who must communicate the following:

(a) name and company of visitor;
(b) status within the company;
(c) objectives of visit;
(d) his value to the supplier: past, present, future;
(e) role of the various individuals involved.

Other factors that need to be borne in mind are:

(a) need to pre-warn staff concerned with reception, switchboard, refreshments;
(b) need to amuse/entertain;
(c) language or cultural factors;
(d) need to impress and acknowledge status;
(e) involvement of employees with similar interests;
(f) the feminine touch.

8.4 TRAINING NEEDS

It cannot be assumed that all company personnel will automatically possess the wide variety of skills and knowledge required to deal with major customers.

The salesman may be well trained to carry out the traditional sales interview but can he (a) negotiate, (b) ask relevant questions and use the answers, (c) analyse financial problems, (d) calculate financial benefits, (e) read a profit and loss account, (f) work out a customer strategy, (g) systematically forecast sales, (h) co-ordinate the total activity, (i) influence individuals over whom he has no control, (f) use the customer record system?

Does the applications engineer or quality control manager have (a) the necessary social skills, (b) the sales skills, (c) the presentation ability?

All these and many more training needs must be considered and satisfied. It is important to identify carefully the relevant training needs. This must be done by considering in detail the various parts of the job of dealing with major customers and the levels of knowledge, skills and attitudes required to carry them out effectively. The actual knowledge, skill and attitudes possessed by the individual must then be identified and training provided to close any gap between actual and desired levels.

The training methods will vary depending on individual and company needs. They include:

1 In-company programmes
  (a) run by internal staff,
  (b) conducted by outside consultants.

2   Attendance at public seminars/courses.
3   Written material, e.g. books, publications, programmed learning packages.
    (See Bibliography, p 148.)

These methods are now described in more detail.

In-company programmes

The main advantage of this form of training is that it can be tailored to the unique situation faced by the company. It can take into account the particular needs of the trainees and the requirements of individual customers. For sales staff it may be necessary to divide the training into two modules, the first concentrating on the planning process and the second on effectively handling the major customer and conducting the sales negotiation. Generally the trainees will use the time between the courses (not more than two months) to complete their major customer plans which will be used as a basis for the second module.

Training for the sales support functions generally takes relatively less time and should concentrate on skill development. Use of closed circuit television whereby the individual can see himself as others do can reorient attitudes and skills very quickly. This method is more effective than many hours of formal lecturing.

Frequently, outside consultants are used to conduct this training where the company does not have the required resources.

Public seminars

These are very useful for increasing awareness of the techniques, pitfalls and opportunities. Since delegates will be drawn from a variety of companies and industries, these seminars provide a good opportunity to find out about the variety of approaches being used. However, it is for each individual to relate this back to his own situation. Further, such courses provide little opportunity for the essential skill development needed to handle major customers effectively.

The cost of attending public courses will be considerably less than that of running in-company courses. The time commitment of trainees will also be less.

Written material

There are numbers of books and publications which will be useful in the development of knowledge. Some of the material in this book, such as the contents of this chapter, can be developed by the training manager into learning packages. The effectiveness of this training method is dependent on the time and effort devoted by the individual to understanding the material and developing the application of it to his own circumstances. In addition, this must be reinforced and followed up by his manager using counselling and discussion to make maximum impact.

8.5 SUMMARY

The successful conduct of the ongoing relationship with major customers is *not* something which can be left to chance, on the assumption that everyone involved will do the best they can.

It is important to plan and influence formal and informal customer relationships and to be aware of the stage that the relationship has reached in terms of business development. Where this relationship is maturing then it is vital that the supplier understands and implements the principles and practice of negotiation. This involves detailed preparation and the salesman needs more than ability to 'think on his feet' if he is to be successful in front of the professional buyer. The supplier can lose more profit at this stage than at almost any other. In team negotiation situations, the spokesman may witness his own side giving away large concessions before he can intervene. All members must understand the do's and don'ts of negotiation and the fundamental process of trading concessions.

The support staff are also involved in the relationship and they must be aware of the positive or negative effect they can have on the customer and how they should conduct themselves.

Most organisations are aware of one or more aspects of how to develop their relationships with major accounts. Few are aware of all aspects and even fewer do anything about it in terms of training or systems. Both are vital, particularly training, which must be viewed as a co-ordinated activity across all the relevant staff. Negotiation training for salesmen, effective customer handling training for technical staff, are all very valuable in isolation, but are doubly effective if they are part of a total training plan for all staff, to assist them in handling major customers.

Action planning checklist

	Questions	Answers and action	Timing of action and evaluation
1	How are negotiations planned?		
2	What concessions are frequently given almost as of right which should be negotiated?		
3	What preparation occurs for team negotiation?		
4	What post-negotiation analysis occurs?		
5	What training is given to (a) sales staff? (b) sales support staff?		
6	Is this sufficient?		

9
Controlling the activity

9.1 INTRODUCTION

The best laid plans are subject to the vagaries of individuals, competitors, market forces, etc. Not everything is accurately predictable. The control process is the third element in the objective setting, planning and control discussed in Chapter 5. It involves monitoring actual results against those planned and taking steps to bring the two closer together. In some instances this may mean modifying the plan when, owing to unforeseen events, it has become totally unrealistic. In most cases it will mean changing the activity to achieve the planned results.

This chapter discusses the nature of the control process required for major customers. It is clear that this must be related to the major customer plan and will comprise several parts:

(a) feedback of activity carried out and results achieved;
(b) measurement of actual against planned;
(c) communication of information to individuals to redirect their activities.

Because of the relatively large number of individuals involved it is important to co-ordinate this activity carefully. In Chapter 6 the use of a customer record file was discussed. This can, and should, be extended to become the core of the control system for that customer. It provides the mechanism for bringing together all the activity and results relating to that customer in one document and thus allows analysis of actual against plan, as a result of which corrective action can be taken. The key to effective control is effective communication.

The chapter concerns itself with operational control, i.e. finding out what is happening, rather than managerial or strategic control. It does not look at how in total Mr A or Mr B can work more effectively, but at that part of their work associated with major accounts.

9.2 FEEDBACK OF ACTIVITY AND RESULTS

It is first necessary to establish what activity and which results need to be reported back and to whom. In order to identify the appropriate mechanism answers to the following three questions should be sought.

1 What do we want to achieve?
2 What are the ingredients of success?
3 How should the information be collected?

Results to be achieved

As discussed in Chapter 5, the success of the activity towards major accounts is defined in terms of the achievement of annual profitability and sales objectives. These constitute absolute standards showing what has been achieved at the end of the year with each major customer. Unfortunately, by that time it is probably too late to take corrective action. Thus it is necessary to obtain feedback of results over shorter time periods. For sales this is usually monthly and for profit quarterly, although it may be more frequent. Further useful information will be obtained if the overall sales figure is broken down by volume, value, product, and application, for example. Average order size also provides an interesting statistic.

Profit and sales, however, are only the end result. They cannot be directly controlled. What can and must be controlled are the means by which the results are achieved.

The ingredients of success

In the traditional sales situation the sales manager is concerned that his salesmen call on the desired numbers of customers and prospects, at the right frequency, and carry out effective sales interviews.

With major accounts this becomes more complicated because there are greater numbers of individuals involved, i.e. (a) numerous non-direct sales contacts will occur; (b) the sales process is likely to be lengthy and complex; (c) the types of performance standards will differ amongst different members of the team.

It is necessary to answer four questions to establish meaningful standards:

1 Who has contact with the customer?
2 Why does each person have contact?
3 How frequent is such contact?
4 What occurs during the contact?

Thus, for example, an application engineer may need to have weekly contact with a customer to ensure that his product is successfully installed, modified and operational; the marketing director may be required to make a monthly visit to the customer's managing director to cement senior level relationships; the salesman may have to make a monthly visit to the buyer to ascertain forward requirements and resolve administrative problems.

Besides call frequency, standards may be set for other aspects of the sales process including

(a) number of calls to obtain order;
(b) order/call ratio;
(c) share of customer total purchases;
(d) time spent per call;
(e) sales/sales and service cost ratios;
(f) age of outstanding payments.

Ideally, therefore, standards of performance should be set for each member of the team who has contact with the major customer. In some instances it may be necessary to set standards for individuals who do not have direct contact but whose activity might be crucial, such as draughtsmen. Having decided what particular facets of performance require to be monitored, the major account plan will determine the nature of the standard.

Collecting the information

Deciding on the type and magnitude of performance standards is generally relatively straightforward and the ease with which it is done will increase as the manager gains more practice. Collecting information on actual performance can be much more difficult. Clearly, as with any information system, a compromise has to be made between what is obtainable as compared with what is desirable.

Mechanisms need to be established to allow all contact with the customer to be monitored. How often does the situation arise where, for example, the salesman finds out from the buyer that his marketing director has just visited and agreed new terms, or that the accounts department have agreed to give a credit, or that technical support are putting a man in the customer's factory for two weeks?

Often the problem arises because individuals who have not traditionally been expected to report their activities to each other must now do so. Usually it is the salesman who reports his activities to the marketing director, not the other way round. The technical engineer reports to the technical director normally, not the sales manager. Thus, the effective handling of major accounts crosses the normal line reporting systems within organisations. This is one of the main reasons why many suppliers (a) service major customers poorly, (b) do not attempt to set up the necessary control systems.

To generate the necessary information each company must develop its own reporting procedures and formats. Generally, this will involve everyone who visits the customer reporting back. If a common format can be used so much the better. The example in Figure 9.1 shows a reporting format for inside and outside sales engineers for an industrial company. This is supplemented by the call report form shown in Figure 9.2 which is used by all other staff who contact the customer. It is difficult to limit completion of these forms to major customers only, since it would mean sales staff and others completing the forms on some occasions and not on others. This can create considerable confusion and it is generally the case that all calls are reported irrespective of the nature of the customer. It is then up to the office to extract information which is relevant to major customers. A typical example of the salesman reporting format used in the fast-moving consumer goods industry is shown in Figure 9.3.

In both cases (Figures 9.1 and 9.3) it will be noted that codings are used to obtain particular information. In the consumer example they represent different types of promotional activity, particular product sales and the recording of specific customer information. In the industrial sales engineer reporting forms (Figure 9.1) the numbers refer to the stage that a particular project has reached. In turn this enables a project record card, shown in Figure 9.4, to be updated so that the status of any particular project with that customer can be obtained at a glance.

Some form of coding is usually necessary if information of what occurred during the call is to be obtained in a standardised manner. Although it is perfectly feasible for the supplier's representative to report everything that occurred on his visit in long hand, or on tape – and some companies still adhere to this practice – it is both time consuming and difficult to analyse. Therefore, it is important to consider in detail the nature of the interaction between each individual and the customer and split this into a number of distinct steps. For example, the job of the technical support manager for an agricultural equipment supplier consisted of the following nine elements:

1   Establish contact with farm owner, manager and machine operator.
2   Obtain details of non-standard requirements.
3   Obtain details of major operational problems.
4   Provide problem solution verbally.
5   Obtain samples, etc., for laboratory analysis.
6   Write report.

133

Weekly report form

Engineer _____ Area _____ Week commencing _____

Day	Company name and location	Contact name(s)	CLAS AC / P / D	PERS VIS / TEL CON	COMP INFO / PGC 4	Project no.	Product and applications discussed	PROJECT STAGE 1 to 10	ACT REQ / PGC 3	Remarks and future action

Project stages

CLAS: Classification	PER VIS: Personal visit	1. Initial contract 6. Quote/requote the enquiry
AC: Active customer	TEL CON: Telephone conversation	2. Identification of decision-makers 7. Follow up quote
P: Prospect	ACT REQ: Action request	3. Pre-enquiry discussions 8. Obtain order
D: Dormant customer		4. Obtain unofficial/budget enquiry 9. Follow up order
		5. Obtain official/firm enquiry 10. Order

Figure 9.1   Weekly sales engineer report form

```
                        Call report form

Customer name _____          Contact made by
and address   _____          _____
              _____
              _____

Customer contact(s)                    Date of call
Name and position(s)_____      _____
              _____
              _____
              _____
```

Nature and objective of contact

Summary of activity

Results achieved

Action to be taken by yourself

By salesman

By office

Other information, for example, competitive activity, trading situation.

Figure 9.2   Reporting format for non-sales staff

Daily report form

No. ___

Salesman ___

Name	District	Type of outlet				No. of cases merchandised			D.L cases on promotion						7 G	8 N	9 AW	10 LP	11	12	13 OP	If applic. NEW A/C	Total cases	Date
		M	I	C+/S+C/M	S/SC/S	O	Mass (10+)	D/B	Shelf	1	2	3	4	5	6										
1																									
2																									
3																									
4																									
5																									
6																									
7																									
8																									
9																									
10																									
11																									
12																									
13																									
14																									
15																									
16																									
17																									
18																									
19																									
20																									
Direct orders only																									
Day's totals																									
Totals b/fwd																									
Totals to date																									

Speedo reading

Start ___

Finish ___

Complete on Friday
Total calls
Total orders
Non-prod. calls?
Av. per order

Figure 9.3 Daily report form

Project card

Company ___
Address ___
___
___

Project potential ___ ASE

Project ref.no. ___

Closing dates
Quotation ___
Validity ___
Order ___

	Value	Date
Quote no. ___	___	___
Order no. ___	___	___
	Delivery date	___

Contact ___
Position ___

DM/INFL ___

Date	Customer contact	Contact made by	Stage of project										Remarks/future action
			1 Initial contact	2 Identify decision makers	3 Pre-enquiry discussions	4 Obtain unofficial/budget enquiry	5 Obtain official/firm enquiry	6 Quote/requote sent/received	7 Follow-up quote	8 Obtain order	9 Follow-up order	10 Other	

Figure 9.4 Project card

7 Return visit to present report.

8 Assist in making necessary modifications on site.

9 Return visit to check progress.

The nine steps are coded 1 to 9 and the technical support manager will put the appropriate number on the form. This does not mean that each step must be tackled consecutively. From previous visits he may already have accomplished step 1, quickly carry out step 2, jump to step 4 and then straight to step 8 all in one visit.

To bring together all activity relating to a major customer in a summary form it is necessary to keep a customer record card for each account. The examples shown in Figures 9.5 and 9.6 are for an industrial goods supplier and a catering supplier respectively. This record card is vitally important since it provides basic customer details and summary of historical purchases, both being essential requirements if realistic forecasting and objective setting is to take place.

Each company must set up its own system for collecting the necessary information about the activity towards, and results achieved from, major customers. The examples discussed demonstrate that there are a multiplicity of possible formats and that there is no 'best' layout for all possible situations.

In setting up the major account control system, the manager should carry out the following steps.

1 Identify and define a clear set of activity and result standards for the customer and each person involved with the customer.

2 Ascertain who needs what information and how quickly after the event.

3 Bring together all systems and forms currently being used.

4 Modify and utilise existing systems wherever possible.

5 Develop new formats as appropriate.

6 Assess feasibility of the new system working effectively.

7 Modify system to make it workable, if necessary, and redefine standards accordingly.

With the increase in information now available as a result of computerisation, it is a good rule before any information is ever collected about any aspect of business to ask these questions:

1 What decision has to be taken?

2 Within what degree of accuracy?

3 How quickly?

and then to ask

4 What information is necessary?

5 From whom should it be collected?

6 How should it be collected?

9.3 MEASURING ACTUAL PERFORMANCE AGAINST PLANNED

Up to now a picture has been painted of numbers of pieces of paper (forms) flowing hither and thither containing much information. For this data to be of use it must be collated and analysed. The way in which this is generally done is by comparing actual performance against plan or budget. The difference between actual achievement and budget, plan or standard is the variance. A simple example of how such a system would work is shown in Figure 9.7.

Customer record card

Date of next call _____   Application _____   Product _____

Company _____
Address(es) _____
Application/industry _____
Tel. no. _____   Position _____   Area code(s) _____

Contact Name(s) _____   Comments _____   DM/INFL _____

Products produced or services sold _____

Products suitable _____

Potential order over 5 years _____

Date	Type of call		Quotations issued		Order received		Order lost			General comments and information
	Pers.	Tel.	Number	Value	Number	Number	Number	To whom	Why	
Total										
Total										
Total										
Total										
Total										

Figure 9.5   Customer record card

Customer record card

Phone no. Contact Designation

Invoice address

Delivery address (if different)

Staff no:-
Machine no.
Models:
Snack potential:

			Small cups	Large cups	Caster sugar	Milk	Tea	Coffee	Carb. drinks	Soft drinks					No. of cases
		Items													
		Brand													
		Prices													
Date	Customer order no.	Our order no.													

Figure 9.6 Customer record card

---

1 The salesman completes his daily call report form and returns a copy to the office.
2 The office updates their major customer record card to show a visit has been made.
3 The number of calls made is totalled at the end of each month.
4 A summary is prepared at the end of each month by the office of actual calls made against plan.

Figure 9.7   Call frequency

A similar procedure is followed for each of the standards set, with the received data being accumulated under various headings as appropriate. All this collated data can then be brought together in a key account summary form. An example, from a food manufacturing organisation is shown in Figure 9.8 which summarises results and activity against plan on a rolling monthly basis. The defined standards in this case are: (a) volume sales by product group; (b) stock/order ratio by product group; (c) number of shelf facings obtained by product group; (d) volume of merchandising by product group; (e) promotion volume; (f) new lines introduced; (g) number of sales calls; (h) number of orders; (i) order to call ratio; (j) time spent in store. Every three months this information is supplemented by the addition of a customer profit and loss account comparing actual against budget.

Clearly there is considerable value in getting this type of data processing computerised and this is becoming increasingly common. However, it is undoubtedly wise when initially setting up such a system to do the processing manually since it tends to be easier to smooth out any initial difficulties.

9.4   REDIRECTION OF ACTIVITIES

When the actual performance deviates too much from that planned, corrective action must be taken. This presupposes that a certain amount of variance is acceptable and that action need only be taken when performance moves outside these limits as shown in Figure 9.9. An upper and lower control limit are established and only when the actual achievement falls outside, as in periods 3, 8 and 9, will it be necessary to consider taking rectifying action. Managers will normally be attuned to negative variances, i.e. sales below budget, average order size below plan, call rate below plan, but less frequently to positive variances, often feeling that this is positively beneficial to the company. This need not be the case and often is not, for example, substantial over-achievement on, say, average order size may cause strain on the production function or exceeding the sales budget significantly may lead to over-trading.

In deciding on the appropriate corrective action, the financial effect of the alternatives can be evaluated using the profit and loss account. This may be straightforward or quite complex.

A typical illustration is that of a supplier of industrial consumables achieving his sales volume budget but at reduced prices and failing to meet his profit objectives.

To rectify this situation a number of alternatives exist, including these ten possibilities.

1 Increase prices by reducing discounts. This would work if volume can be maintained.
2 Redirect sales effort to higher margin lines. This will have a cost since some sort of sales incentive will be required for the salesmen.

Key account summary

Name _____
Address _____

Planned calls ———— No. order obtained ———— Actual ———— Planned
Actual calls ———— Order: call ————

Month ———— Actual ———— Planned
Time spent

Product groups	Month 1 Stock/ order S	2 S/O	S	3 S/O	S	4 S/O	S	5 S/O	S	6 S/O	S	7 S/O	S	8 S/O	S	9 S/O	S	10 S/O	S	11 S/O	S	12 S/O	S	Average S/O	S	Target S/O	S
Sales 1																												
2																												
3																												
4																												
5																												
6																												
7																												

Facing Volume merchandising	M	F	M	F	M	F	M	F	M	F	M	F	M	F	M	F	M	F	M	F	M	F	M	F	V	F	V	F
1																												
2																												
3																												
4																												
5																												
6																												
7																												

Promotions volume product code

New lines product code

Figure 9.8 Monthly key account summary

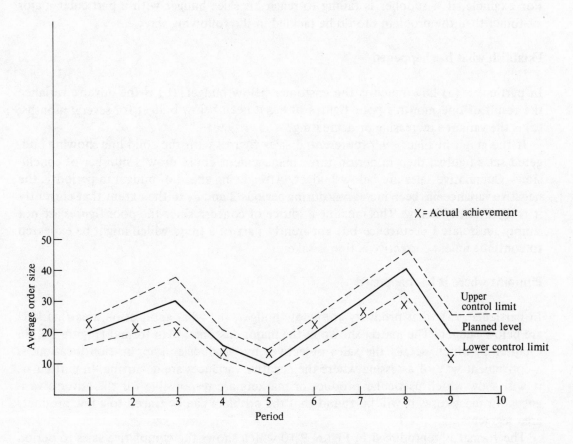

Figure 9.9 Control limits

3 Reduce prices further but this is viable only if increased sales exceed reductions offered and production has capacity to supply.

4 Promote higher margin lines: offer additional discounts on these lines to increase sales at overall higher average gross margin.

5 Increase call rate on customer, and hence increase sales.

6 Negotiate contract order.

7 Invite key customer contact to works visit.

8 Reduce call rate, and hence sales costs.

9 Reduce technical support, and hence costs.

10 Reduce customer entertainment, and hence costs.

Each of the possibilities can be costed and the effect on the profit and loss account for this customer evaluated. As a result it may be judged that a combination of measures is required.

In order to assess which measures are most likely to rectify the adverse variances, it is useful to adopt a five stage approach.

1 Identify what has happened.

2 Identify where it has happened.

3 Assess why it has happened.

4 Determine corrective action.

5 Implement the action and monitor results.

For example, if a supplier is failing to reach his sales budget with a particular major customer then the problem should be tackled in the following way.

Establish what has happened

In particular, (a) how much is the customer below budget; (b) is the adverse variance the result of one month's poor figures or has it been below budget for several months; (c) is the variance increasing or decreasing?

If the graph in Figure 9.9 represented sales figures with the solid line showing budgeted sales figures, then in period three management could draw a number of conclusions. Cumulative sales are below budget. After being ahead of budget in period 1, the negative variance has been increasing during periods 2 and 3, to the extent that currently it is significantly below. This must be a source of concern since the poor figures are not simply an isolated occurrence but apparently part of a trend which might be expected to continue unless corrective action is taken.

Pinpoint where it has happened

In particular, (a) what products are below budget; (b) what application/areas/markets are below budget? The matrix shown in the major customer plan format (Figure 5.2) in Chapter 5, which details the sales objectives by product and application/location, is a convenient way of assessing where the negative variances are occurring. In particular, it will show which particular product or markets are responsible for the adverse variances. In most cases it will be found that the problem can be traced to a few product/area segments.

The format is reproduced in Figure 9.10 which shows the cumulative sales to period 3. The total negative variance £18,360 is mainly as a result of a £13,060 variance in location (a), and a £14,900 variance for product B.

b = budget a = actual £000s			Locations (a)	(b)	(c)	Total	Variance
Products	A	b a	10.00 7.50	12.00 11.83	15.00 15.45	37.00 34.78	(2.22)
	B	b a	6.50 2.15	8.50 3.15	10.00 4.80	25.00 10.10	(14.90)
	C	b a	12.33 6.77	2.30 4.35	6.85 8.22	21.48 19.34	(2.14)
	D	b a	0.80 0.15	1.20 1.80	3.65 4.60	5.65 6.55	0.90
Total		b a	29.63 16.57	24.00 21.13	35.50 33.07	89.13 70.77	
Variance			(13.06)	(2.87)	(2.43)		(18.36)

Figure 9.10 Cumulative sales to period 3 – major customer X

This analysis clearly indicates that management should focus its attention on what is happening in location (a) and product B. The problem is simplified since management does not have to consider all the many aspects of sales to customer X, only two.

Assess why it is happening

The large variances should now be examined in detail to establish the main reasons for them. Sometimes the reason may be simple. For example, the poor performance of product B may be due to production problems which have reduced supply of the product, or it may be as a result of a failure to implement a large price increase. Sometimes the reasons require considerable investigation to identify the real cause of the problem. This may necessitate discussion with the sales personnel concerned and with the customer. A positive and effective informal relationship with the customer can greatly help in these discussions.

Determine corrective action

Having identified the real reasons for the poor performance the supplier should then list the alternative courses of action to bring the major customer back on plan. Each alternative should be costed and the effect on profitability determined. The decision, as to which activities will be most appropriate, is a complex one that should be made with regard to the following criteria:

1. Will it achieve the desired objectives?
2. Does it fit in with overall company policy?
3. How much does it cost?
4. How difficult is it to implement?
5. How much time will it take?

Implement the actions and monitor results

Having decided on the appropriate action this then needs to be communicated to those individuals who must implement it. Again it is often useful to glean their opinion first, thus making them aware of the problem and increasing their commitment to its solution.

9.5 SUMMARY

To set up an effective system for controlling the activity towards, and results achieved with, major customers, the manager must

(a) identify the results and activity that should be measured and the best method to collect the information;
(b) collate and analyse the information collected to enable actual performance to be compared with that planned;
(c) analyse the causes for significant variances between actual and planned performance and take corrective action.

The reporting formats which are completed by the staff who have customer contact will normally need to incorporate some form of coding to ensure that the required information is collected in a standard manner. Collecting information to cover all aspects of performance and results achieved is generally impractical. The managers must, therefore, compromise between what is desirable and what is obtainable.

Having collected the relevant information and compared it against plan significant adverse variances must be corrected by (a) identifying what has happened; (b) pin-pointing where it has happened; (c) assessing why it has happened; (d) determining corrective action; (e) implementing the action and monitoring results.

A difficulty in controlling the performance of major customers is that it generally requires crossing traditional lines of reporting and control. Further, the manager is often trying to obtain information about a part of an individual's activities, whilst the majority of his time may be spent on other matters.